KIND WORDS FOR

Into the Wilds of Parenthood

"It armed me with new-found knowledge and awareness about what to expect, and methods to deal with that, so I was able to replace my apprehension with confidence and felt empowered to begin the journey of Motherhood."

– Michelle W.

"Even though bubba has not been born yet, I feel much more confident for the first few weeks... This is great support!"

– Valeria

"Having moved into the toddler mum stage I'm more focused on the other aspects of my life now but would have loved something like this when I was a new mum!"

– Michelle K.

"Thanks for giving new parents reassurance on their newborn path and not feeling alone along the way."

– Juliette

"I'm a new parent, my daughter is 6 weeks old... I'm so pleased I found this, as so much of what I've been looking at is all about the baby and what she should be doing at each stage. It's so nice to have something that's more focused on what this new journey is like for parents."

– Trina

"I'm so glad this book found me. Especially before I gave birth. This will be my new gift to all mums to be, I couldn't recommend it more!"

– Elena

A catalogue record for this book is available from the National
Library of New Zealand.
Soft cover ISBN 978-1-7386216-0-6
Hard Cover ISBN 978-1-7386216-1-3
Kindle ISBN 978-1-7386216-2-0
epub ISBN 978-1-7386216-3-7
iBook ISBN 978-1-7386216-4-4
Cover design by Pip Findlay
Cover photo from Canva designer @katya-havok
Design & layout by Fiverr designer Hamza Hazeem @hamzahazeem
Printed in New Zealand by www.yourbooks.co.nz
This book has been printed using sustainably managed stock.

INTO THE WILDS
OF PARENTHOOD

THE ULTIMATE SURVIVAL GUIDE FOR NEW MUMS
ENTERING THE WILD WORLD OF PARENTHOOD

PIP FINDLAY
Founder of Wild Beginnings

Contents

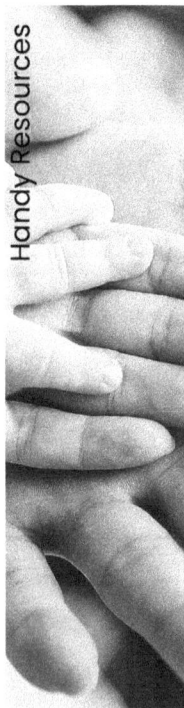

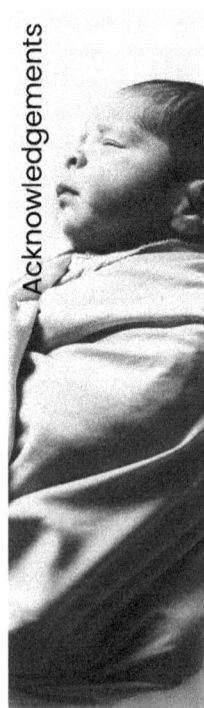

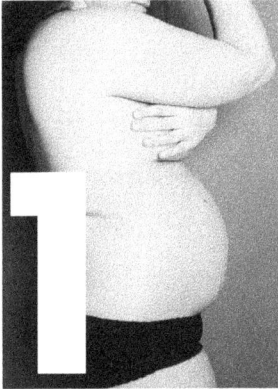

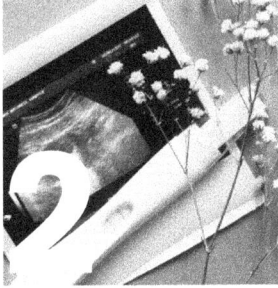

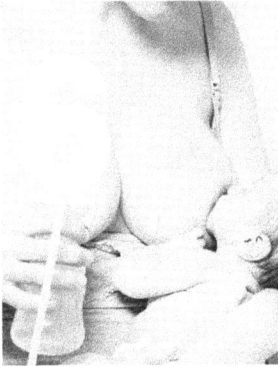

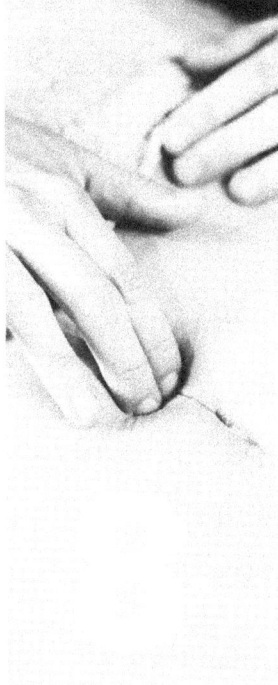

ONE

TWO

THREE

FOUR

FIVE

SIX

SEVEN

EIGHT

NINE

TEN

Introduction

WELCOME TO YOUR PARENTHOOD, YOUR WILD BEGINNING

Dearest mumma,

In the months since you began your pregnancy journey, how many times have you wished for an instruction manual?

I asked myself the same thing, particularly during my first pregnancy.

As a former Early Parenting Educator and the Founder of Wild Beginnings, I've worked with New Zealand's largest Parenting Education organisation, Parents Centre Aotearoa, and hundreds of new parents to help them smoothly transition into parenthood. Parenting is WILD, and you don't know what you don't know.

This book aims to take you through the key things you should be aware of as new parents, but that no one seems to discuss with you before becoming a parent, particularly a mum.

Think of this book as your closest equivalent to a manual for entering parenthood.

> You're about to give birth and raise an infant but you're also in the infancy of your parenting journey. And it can be a really, wild ride, especially in the beginning.

I should however note upfront that this book is NOT about baby. This book will not teach you how to bath or feed baby, discuss co- or sleep training, the signs of tiredness, or how to distinguish whether baby is experiencing colic or reflux.... No. No. No. If you are after these answers, then this is not the book for you, my friend. Too often I hear new parents exclaim (and I too experienced this, hence the very birth of Wild Beginnings itself),

> There is so much information out there for baby, but what about me?!

Yes! This book is about, and I emphasize this, YOU. What, and why, are YOU experiencing what you are as a new parent? What, and why, are YOU feeling the way you do? When will things begin to feel normal again? And most importantly, how do YOU improve your current situation, in the very least being armed with the knowledge to understand why you are encountering the experiences you are, so that you can learn to thrive in your parenthood? THIS is what this book is about.

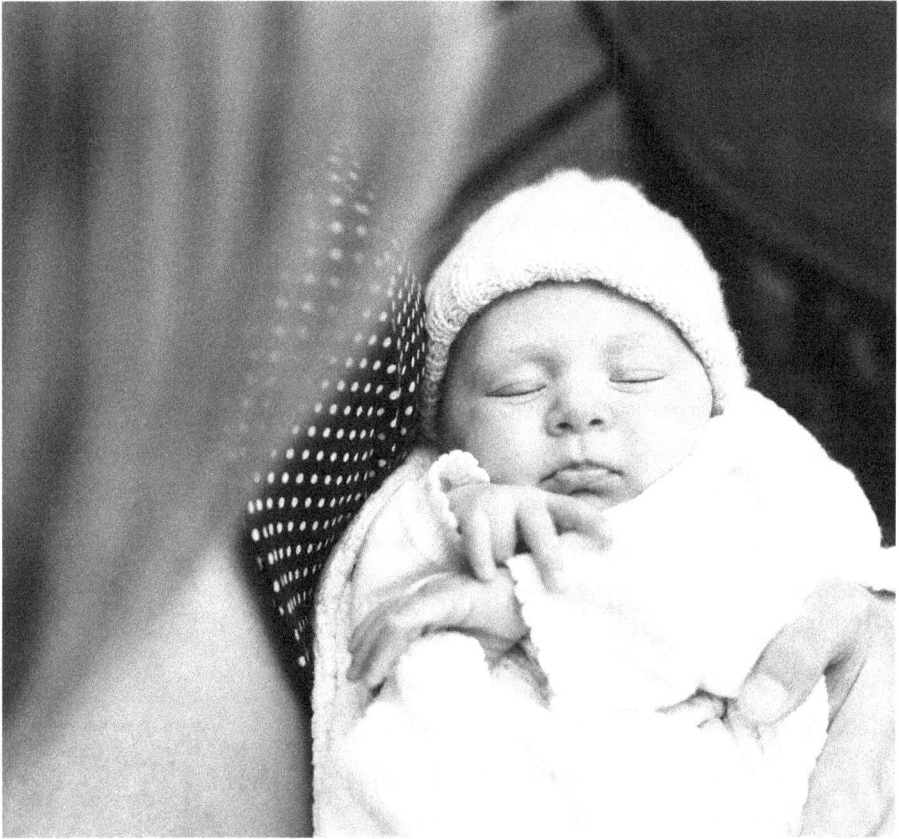

How can we fully serve our family if we cannot begin by supporting and rebuilding ourselves, following the immensely life-changing experience of becoming a parent?

So whether you're pregnant and wanting to ease your anxiety about parenthood, a first time parent with a newborn experiencing the highs and lows that come with parenting, or you're adding to the family and need a bit more support and a postpartum refresher, this book is for you.

I'm excited to walk this wild journey together with you. Thank you for choosing to join me, let's get into it shall we!

With love, Pip x

Founder of Wild Beginnings

Online Courses for You at

wildbeginnings.thinkific.com

Let's get social

@wildbeginningsnz

I'd love to hear from you, email me here

heywildmumma@gmail.com

My
Story

I didn't even know the Fourth Trimester was a thing

Congratulations! You're one step closer towards making a smoother transition into parenthood.

Right now, you're probably feeling anxious, overwhelmed and utterly exhausted. I understand how you're feeling, I've been there. I'm a mum of two, so I empathise with the highs and lows of the complex world of parenthood.

Before becoming a new parent, I thought I was prepared. You name it, I did it - antenatal classes, hypnobirthing classes, countless chats with friends and family, as well as reading dozens of pamphlets from midwives and caring hospital staff.

But, when I entered parenthood, I was in shock. Blissfully unaware, I had opened what felt like Pandora's box. And I wasn't sure how to cope with what was inside.

I realised that I'd spent all my hours of effort in focusing on the birth and on the 'finish line.' Apart from filling up the freezer with a few comforting meals, I didn't focus on the postpartum period.

I certainly didn't concentrate on the Fourth Trimester and beyond. In fact, I didn't even know about it! If it's new to you too, the Fourth Trimester is the first 12 weeks with your newborn. It's the time when they're becoming acquainted with life outside the safe cocoon of the womb, learning to distinguish between day and night, and honing their senses.

> The Fourth Trimester is also our transition into parenthood.

Becoming a parent with Harry, my firstborn, was certainly wild. A baptism by fire, I experienced breastfeeding difficulties, severe recti diastasis and then a stomach hernia as a result of this, haemorrhoids, and months of painful sex up to nine months following birth before seeking treatment. And that's on top of the normal challenges of raising a newborn.

So I sought out trusted parenting experts in both New Zealand and abroad to support ME as the primary caregiver, as mum — to help me to understand what was happening to MY mind and body. I needed guidance on how to achieve peace of mind and learn how to support my postpartum recovery and rebuild myself to better show up for my baby, and my family.

When my daughter Taylor arrived, two years following Harry's birth, I was far better prepared for becoming a mum of two. Although the demands of early parenthood seemed never-ending, and I became quite the expert in running after a toddler while nursing a newborn, I didn't experience the same shock I'd had with Harry.

BECOMING A NEW PARENT IS EXCITING, THRILLING, LIFE-CHANGING AND INCREDIBLY SPECIAL. IT IS HARD, BUT IT SHOULDN'T BE AS HARD AS WE TEND TO ACCEPT. WE SHOULDN'T BE NORMALISING SO MANY OF THE CHALLENGES WE ARE FACED WITH.

-Pip Findlay

It can appear that all the information out there is directed towards your baby, but there is SO much support for us as parents ourselves. I wish I'd known where to get help, who to have talked to, what to expect, and what questions to ask as a first-time parent.

Instead, I was suffering with terrible physical and mental pain in what should have been the most empowering period of my life. I was intimidated to ask 'embarrassing' questions about what I was experiencing, not knowing what to ask an 'expert,' and who I could talk to in the first place.

It was an isolating period, feeling that I was the only one experiencing certain moments and challenges. There was the confusion that came with receiving contradictory advice (thanks to 3am Googling sessions and unsolicited advice!). I was feeling overwhelmed and unable to distinguish what was 'normal,' I had constant anxiety in worrying about my baby, coupled with guilt that I wasn't doing enough for bubs. Not to mention the utter exhaustion of the infinite list of household tasks between nappy changes, feeds, my own rest, and navigating how relationships, including the one with my partner, were gradually changing around me.

AND SO WE BUILD THIS COMMUNITY, WHERE POSTPARTUM SUPPORT AND EDUCATION ISN'T NEGLECTED, IT'S JUST A GIVEN.

-Shelly Mackie, Postpartum Doula

I believe being well equipped with the knowledge about the challenges to experience in entering parenthood will even help to reduce the rate of postpartum depression. Because knowledge is power. Being armed with this knowledge fuels awareness. Better awareness sets realistic self-expectations. And realistic self-expectations empower us.

Congratulations for being here.

This is your opportunity to gain a better awareness about what's to come in your Fourth Trimester and your early parenting days. You'll discover where to seek help, who exists out there to talk to amongst your loved ones, and be encouraged to go out and seek any additional support you may need.

This is the start of your parenting journey, of your wild beginning. Let's make it an empowering, confident, and smooth transition for you. You deserve it.

Value from this book

LEARN FROM THE EXPERTS & TRUSTED RESOURCES

I want this book to be the cushion to your fall, the parachute to your skydive.

> **Parenthood will land you in the deep end, but this is your buoy and beacon.**

This book will provide you with the awareness you need to understand what's happening to your body and mind and the enormity of the hormonal shifts you'll experience within just 24 hours after giving birth to your bundle.

> **There is no perfect parent, baby, or way of parenting, and in fact embracing the wild imperfections is a GOOD thing.**

There is no need to follow this book from start to finish, or to read it all in one go. Simply choose the chapter that resonates with you at the time and focus on one thing that is meaningful to you at that point in time.

There is so much information to absorb at a period when it's near impossible to keep your eyes open, so don't add pressure onto yourself in feeling that you have to complete this book or tick it off before baby comes. This book is designed to empower you, not to make you feel guilty for reading bits and pieces as you go. It is always here for you and you can continue to refer to your postpartum period, beyond your Fourth Trimester.

Having sought out trusted experts within the parenting field, I've included the support they offered me within this book. I've summarised their information and resources to support you, so you know that you're getting information and guidance from the very best – without having to pay an arm and a leg. Most importantly, you'll understand how they can best help you if you choose to seek treatment from them, while knowing what to expect and what questions to ask them.

The experts I've compiled information from include a **naturopathic doctor focusing on women's hormones, a pelvic floor therapist, a nutritionist, a doula,** and the **founder of a lactation blends business.** Most importantly, you'll also get to hear **stories and advice from several mums** who just like you, were once beginners learning to find their feet and brace the wild unknown of parenthood.

You can sit in the comfort of your own home, take in the information at your own pace and take in what YOU want to take in. **At the end of the book, a list of helpful resources is provided.** Further, if you're after additional support, you can check out **wildbeginnings.thinkific.com for online courses with videos and resources from myself and the experts mentioned within this book.**

I want to help you to become aware of the challenges that mums universally experience in the transition into motherhood, and how to overcome them, so that you can confidently grow into loving your motherhood journey.

It's normal to find the transition difficult, it's normal to not love every day of motherhood and it's normal to feel more overwhelmed than you've ever been in your life.

> Awareness of why you're experiencing and feeling what you are, together with helpful tools to support you and knowing who's out there to help you in your early parenting journey, will lead to a smoother postpartum recovery.

The ride will always be a wild one, and there will be bumps along the road, but you'll be able to anticipate them and be better prepared to avoid them.

Walking into the wild together

It is our village, our mother peers, our partners, our family, our friends, and colleagues, who will play a vital role in our mental wellbeing and support us along this new path.

Know that whatever you're experiencing, somewhere another mother is facing just what you are.
You are never alone.

I want this book to serve as a reminder of that, propped up on your bedside table when you're doing a 3am morning feed.

So, let's get started.

Welcome to days filled with more joy and confidence in your parenting journey!

CHAPTER
ONE
Your Postpartum

A RECIPE FOR POSTPARTUM SUCCESS

Key Ingredients for a smooth transition into your postpartum days

Prior to becoming a parent, you're likely to be preoccupied with making sure the car seat is installed, purchasing the latest baby gadgets (who agrees with me, buying a pram is like buying a car!), preparing the nursery, and spending much time packing and repacking every item in the hospital bag. And of course, the fun events like a baby shower. Enjoy these things!

When you enter the postpartum phase, you gradually realise the importance of honouring this period.

"OH, THE THINGS I WISH I'D KNOWN!..."

In the postpartum phase, you'll learn to come to terms with the fact that parenting is going to be wild. And that you'll need support, love, and touch from others, just as much as your baby relies on you. Your village will become your cornerstone in raising your child.

Finding your village

How can you access what you need from your loved ones, especially if they don't live near you? This is the time to consider your communities, other new parents, and other caring individuals and organisations that you can turn to. **See "How to Build your Village" on page 39 at the end of this chapter.**

When it comes to rebuilding yourself, there are many experts in the parenthood field that focus on your wellbeing as the primary caregiver, including your lead maternity carer, birth trauma counsellors, pelvic floor therapists, lactation consultants and doulas to support and care for you, to name a few.

If you need help, I bet your bottom dollar there's somebody there for you. That's what led me on my path to helping new parents and working with the different experts that exist in this field. There is support for YOU (and not just baby as it may feel), you don't need to ever feel alone.

Why do you need support postpartum?

Did you know that in the Third Trimester your brain shifts and structurally changes? It physiologically gears you into becoming a parent, so you're dealing not only with a physical change but with a mental shift. The medical term for this is known as mumnesia, but we better know it as 'mumbrain.' See, it's a real thing! Don't be so hard on yourself the next time you try to put the open milk in the pantry instead of the fridge, or when you forget the simplest of things such as your pet's name (speaking from experience here...).

That's why during the postpartum period, it's important to rebuild our brain just as we rebuild our hormone balance. And often we feel that we're not doing a perfect job.

Remember, you're doing absolutely everything that you can, and **it's perfectly normal to feel imperfect**. We should embrace the imperfections that come with parenting because no human being is perfect.

> Snowflakes are imperfect. They're all different. Every leaf on a tree is different. I go back to nature just to show how nature is imperfect, but so beautiful. And that's exactly what parenting is like.

There are many challenges we face as new parents, and as mothers, our bodies and minds go through the ringer! But things will improve, and I promise you this, you and your baby will both find your way.

I'm passionate about talking about the wildness of parenthood.

Embrace the wildness, embrace the imperfections and you're one step closer to easing your anxiety and enjoying the wild, beautiful ride that you're on!

THE FIVE PILLARS OF POSTPARTUM

1

EXTENDED REST

2

COMMUNITY

3

NUTRITION AND WARMTH

4

LOVING TOUCH

5

CONNECTION TO NATURE

You've got this mumma!

Postpartum is a time of adapting to parenthood and your new self-identity, capability, and confidence as a mother. You'll be adjusting to changes in your relationships with others, including your partner, and learning how to navigate the 'new normal' of parenthood. These five pillars are a useful guide as you walk down your postpartum path.

① Extended rest

The act (or the art!) of lying in with your baby for 40 days after birth is practised in many cultures around the world, particularly the Eastern cultures. This is a time where you can learn your baby's cues, heal your body, and spend time together as a new family.

Too often today in our Western world, resting for 40 days may not only sound impractical, but it may not be a realistic option from a financial standpoint, and from the immediate support offered around us.

The point is, rest is important. It is part of the healing process. While you may not be able to rest for a set 40 days with your bundle, try to ease the load on yourself. For example, can you steer clear on big trips to the supermarket, rather opting for grocery deliveries, or picking up the essentials from a nearby convenience store (even better, asking a loved one to assist with this)? Can you avoid carrying heavy loads of laundry in the first few weeks if you can, and rather pick up fewer items at a time as you move around?

And while it's near impossible to "sleep when the baby sleeps," **read up '9 ways to improve your sleep' at the end of the chapter** – if just one or two tips can assist you, it may very well make the world of difference. If all else fails, remember that everything is just a phase, and the beautiful 'Mother's love story on sleep' towards the end of the chapter should help to provide some comfort. You've got this mumma, and you are doing an incredible job!

② Community

Culturally and historically, it would be a collection of wise women that understand the postpartum period and support you in that space.

These days, your community could be family, it could be a wise woman around you. It could be your friends, it could be your hairdresser, or the local grocer that knows you by name and asks after you and has everything ready for you.

> **Community is important, but importantly it's those individuals that you want around you during your postpartum days.**

Don't feel obliged to welcome every Tom, Dick, and Harry into your home to meet the baby. Give yourself time, focus on your energy reserves, and let in those that will support YOU. **See "How to Build your Village" on page 39 at the end of this chapter.**

(3) Nutrition and warmth

We need deeply nutritious food. Ideally, slow-cooked, warm food that's high in good fats, herbs and spices that will nourish and restore our joints, organs, and our brain.

Our brain is going through a rapid transformation, and our brains are mainly comprised of fat, so we need nutritious fats to help us rebuild our brain. Foods with Omega 3 fatty acids are supportive in doing this, allowing you to avoid #mumbrain – but it's always a handy excuse, as and when you need! **Be sure to read up on Postpartum Nutrition in Chapter 7 on page 147**. There are some handy postpartum recipes for you!

(4) Loving touch

Loving touch is just what it says it is, feeling loved through touch. This itself looks different for everyone. It could be snuggling your precious baby. It could be skin-to-skin touch. It could be a deep, warm hug from someone that you love and trust. It could be the warmth of being in someone's company. It could be holding your partner's hand. It could even be body work such as Yoga or Pilates, or massage. It could be cuddles with your furbaby. It could be many beautiful different things depending on what 'touch' it is that you need.

⑤ Connection to nature

Connection to nature could be as simple as setting up your nursing station by a window with a view. It could be beautiful herbal salts to bath in. It could be walking on the beach or feeling the sand between your toes. It could be gardening or picking flowers to bring inside. A connection to nature is nurturing. And it can look very different, again, for different people.

Educate To Empower

Throughout this process, educating the people around you of your needs as a person is important. Friends who have never had a baby may not know how to support you in this period and they may be shy about offering help.

Having discussions with your family and friends and setting expectations of how they should be supporting you in this period is so important. It leads to empowering them as well, because everyone loves you and wants to be there for you.

> By addressing what is important to you, your community will be able to better support you, and become an advocate for future parents in need. And so we build this community, where postpartum support and education isn't neglected, it's just a given.

- Doula, Shelly Mackie

Look after yourself at this pivotal time of parenthood. The road may have a few bumps along the way, but if you focus on including the above in your daily life, I promise you that joy and beauty is just around the corner!

9 WAYS TO IMPROVE SLEEP

Those zzzz are important!

1
SOCIAL MEDIA CAN WAIT

Yes, it can. And so can responding to all those sweet messages from loved ones. Also stop playing the comparison game, mumma.

2
LOWER EXPECTATIONS

You are a parent now. The house is a bombsite. This too is a phase of your life. Let it go, and don't discount the power of a nap.

3
HIDE THE LAUNDRY BASKET

'Sleep when the baby sleeps.' And then you rush for the washing. Hide the laundry basket. There. Easy. Now sleep.

4
FOCUS ON NOURISHMENT

Don't strive for perfect nutrition, but focus on nourishing yourself. Water & iron help to transport oxygen to the brain and combat fatigue.

5
GET SOME FRESH AIR AND BREATHE

Try and incorporate some physical activity into your daily routine, and if possible, not too close to bed time. Breathe. Pause. Reset.

6
SPLIT DUTIES

If possible, try and work out a routine with your loved one(s) to care for the baby so you can both (all) get adequate rest.

7
ITS OK TO BE SELFISH

Have guests coming around? Ask them to help out around the house, or hold the baby so you can rest for a bit. Try not to substitute caffeine for rest!

8
DARK AND COOL

Concentrate on making your bedroom an ideal sleep envoirnment. A dark, cool room will set you up for sleep success - quality over quantity! White noise can help too. (for you and baby)

9
SEEK HELP

If you are still struggling, or are experiencing insomnia, chat with your trusted health professional to seek appropriate treatment.

A MOTHER'S LOVE STORY ON SLEEP

"It won't stay this way forever"

"He's still so little lovely. I promise he will start to get longer chunks of sleep soon, it won't stay this way forever!

You are teaching him you are always there, that being his mum doesn't end at 8pm and start again at 6am. You are showing him that night-time can be a time of peace and relaxation, not something to fear and avoid.

You are helping reduce cortisol levels every time you help him settle in the night, so that one day, he will be able to emotionally regulate himself. You are flooding him with oxytocin every time you hold him close, so that his brain grows more neural connections during sleep and helps consolidate his learning from that day.

I know it's tough, mumma, and I know it's hard when you hear people telling you to sleep train (you don't need to!) or that he needs to be 'self-soothed' (myth!), or that he really should be sleeping in longer chunks by now (he shouldn't).

You are a wonderful mummy, following your best instincts."

– Siobhan, mumma of Josh & Harper, Wirral, UK

HOW TO BUILD YOUR VILLAGE

Finding your Community

Baby Groups and Playgroups

- Parenting organisations
(in New Zealand: Parents Centre, Plunket, YMCA and The Parenting Place are just a few wonderful organisations to turn to for support)
- Your local library
(many libraries offer baby-related activities for mums to engage with each other, and for babies to be exposed to new experiences such as 'Wriggle & Rhyme' or Storytime)
- Kid-friendly cafes and local parks
- Baby-related organisations
(In New Zealand: Space, Baby Sensory, Sign & Rhyme, and Mainly Music are some)
- Swimming classes for little ones
(some swimming lessons are offered for babies from 3 months of age)
- Postnatal Yoga Classes (Baby & Me)
- Baby Massage
- Babywearing dance classes

Mum Groups

- Form a coffee group through antenatal classes (many organisations can place you in a coffee group once you've had bubs, even if you didn't partake in the antenatal classes with them beforehand)
- Postnatal groups where mums can freely offload about all their new motherly experiences
- Mum support groups such as breastfeeding or babywearing support

Social Media

- Facebook Communities (search mum community groups in your local area, and don't forget to join our **Wild Beginnings Facebook group at @wildbeginningsnz** – we're waiting to say hi!)
- Peanut App is a safe online space to ask questions, find support and connect with other women.
- Set up a Whatsapp group with your new mum friends to stay in touch, and to be able to message each other during the wee hours of the morning when it's just you and bubs awake in the household

Perinatal Support

- Your Lead Maternity Carer and GP can direct you to local support services (in New Zealand: recommended organisations include Perinatal Anxiety and Depression Aotearoa (PADA), Mothers' Helpers, Plunket, and Parents Centre Aotearoa)
- A Doula can offer postpartum support through helping to take care of your baby, cook nutritious meals for your family, offer you postpartum massages. Basically, be your mother when you need to be mothered!

Be open-minded

- Be brave, open up and talk about your experiences, you're not alone
- Suggest going out for a night off baby duties with your (new) mum friends
- Offer to volunteer at a baby class
- Add your play dates and coffee catchups to your phone calendar, and motivate yourself to head out – you'll be thankful you did!

QUESTIONS TO ASK FOR YOUR POSTPARTUM VISITS

You can use this checklist below to assist in preparing for visits with your healthcare providers.

PAIN RELIEF – MIDWIFE/ GP/LACTATION CONSULTANT

- ☐ What can I do for pain relief?
- ☐ Any medications to avoid if breastfeeding?
- ☐ Other recommended supplements?
- ☐ How do I know if I'm experiencing constipation or have hemorrhoids?

CONTRACEPTION – MIDWIFE/ GP/LACTATION CONSULTANT

- ☐ Which birth control is safest for me?
- ☐ What to look out for in hormonal changes? My period? Bleeding?
- ☐ Planning to breastfeed or not?
- ☐ Hormonal changes to expect?

MENTAL WELLBEING – MIDWIFE/GP/ SPECIALISED ORGANISATIONS

- ☐ Discussing your emotions
- ☐ Free lines to call for support/people (eg life coach for mums/psychologist etc) to see – specifically new mother focused
- ☐ Recommended local mum groups

EXERCISE - PELVIC FLOOR PHYSIO/POSTNATAL CERTIFIED PT'S

☐ When can I start exercising?

☐ Anything exercise-wise to avoid?

☐ Is my recti-diastasis close to 'normal'? How can I support my core?

☐ Am I doing my kegels right?

☐ What should I expect when I'm ready to start having sex again?

BREASTFEEDING - LACTATION CONSULTANT

☐ What pain is 'normal'?

☐ How do I know when I should seek medical help (eg. mastitis /fungal/ bacterial issue)

☐ Any supportive groups/ and products recommended?

NUTRITION - NUTRITIONIST/DOULA/ GP

☐ Foods to support hormonal regulation?

☐ Foods to combat constipation or hemorrhoids?

☐ Nutrients to support breastfeeding?

Always discuss your personal requirements with your healthcare providers.

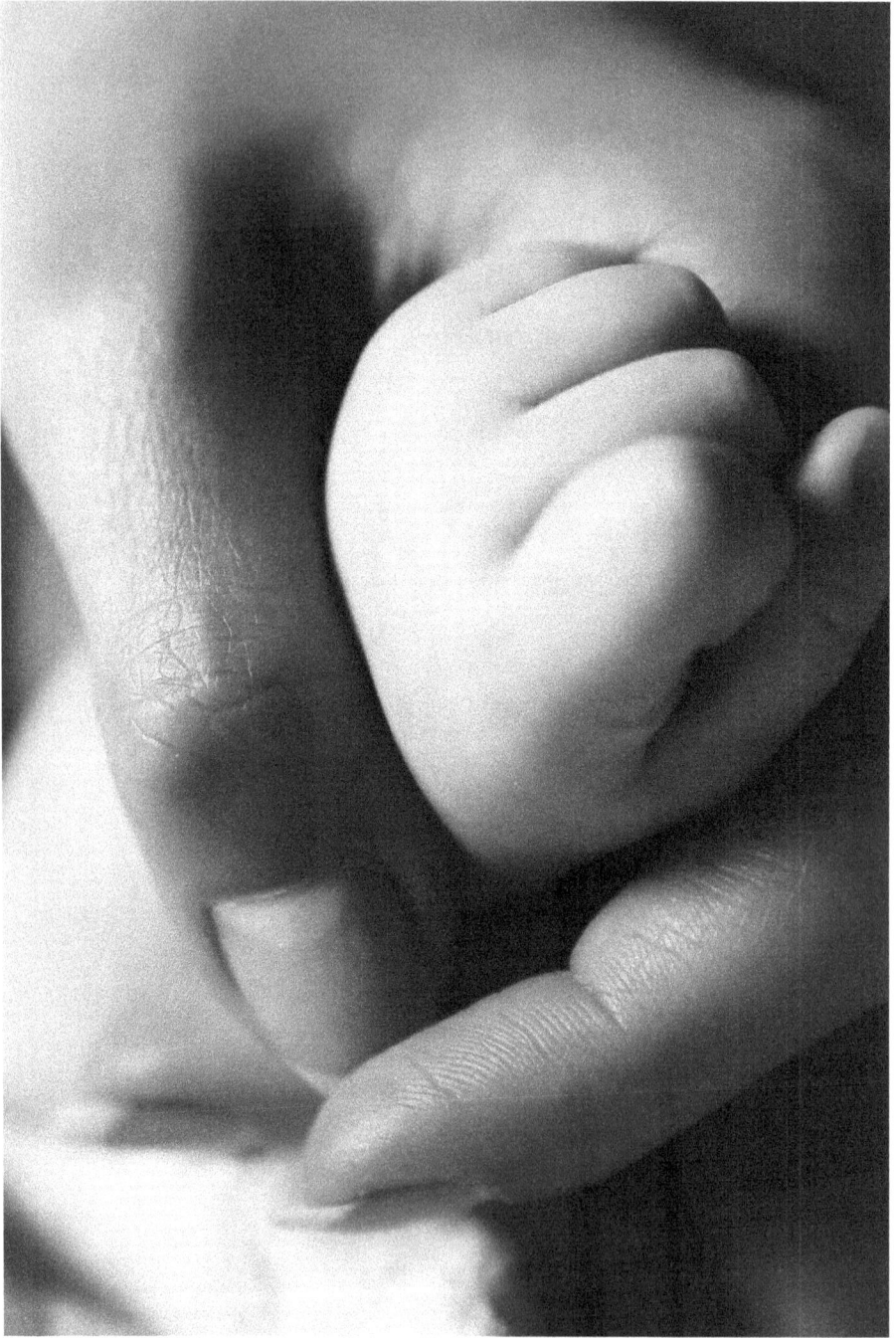

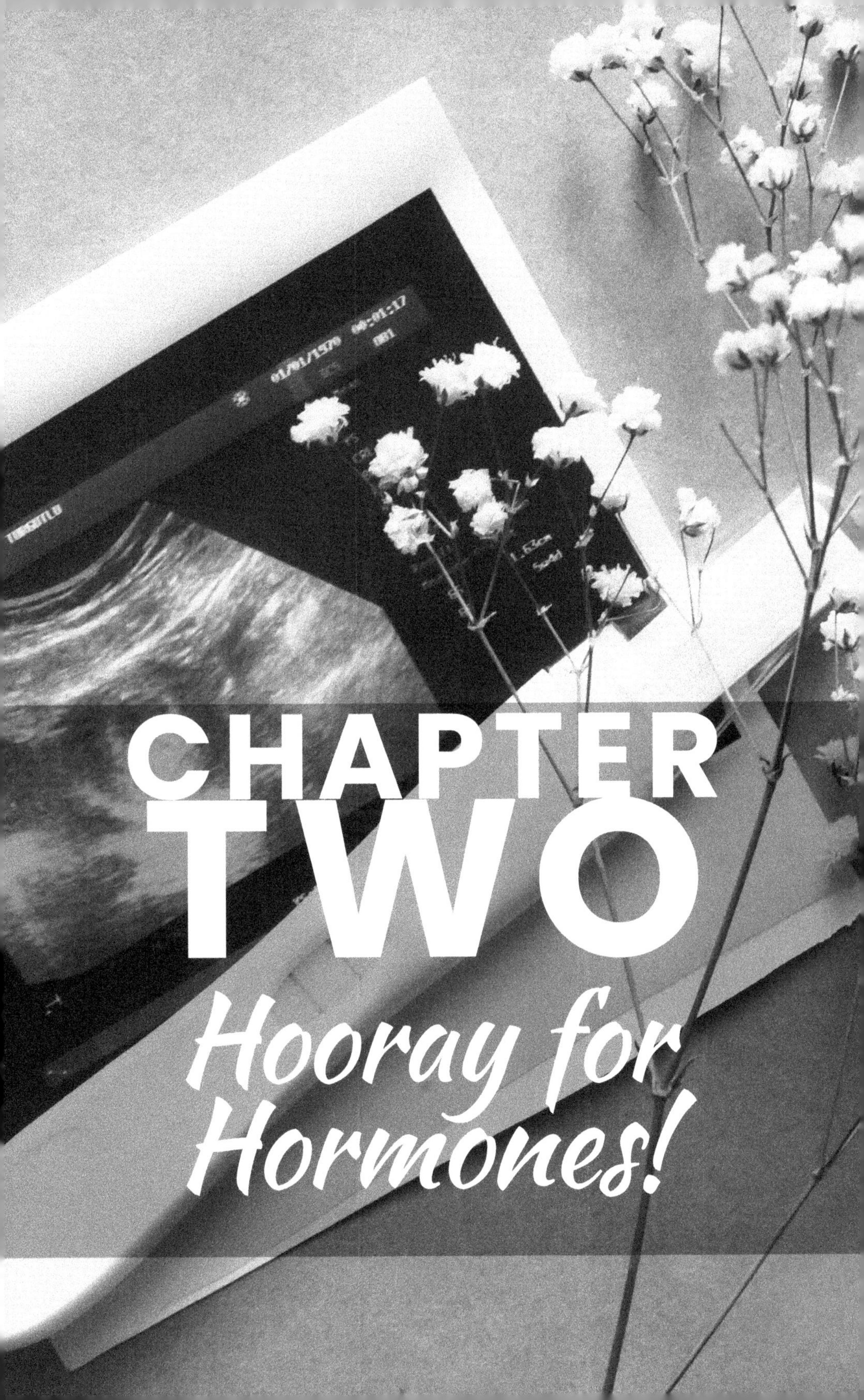

CHAPTER TWO

Hooray for Hormones!

UNDERSTANDING YOUR WILD POSTPARTUM HORMONES

You're not crazy, mumma!

"Generally, around the 6-week mark (when the positive birth hormones have drastically decreased), the signs of postpartum depression can start to creep in, so seek help if you feel you aren't coping. It is important to note that postpartum depression can onset at any time but is relatively common in the transition around 6 weeks."

– Dr Sarah Wilson, Naturopathic Doctor.

Specialized in Women's Hormones & Founder of Advanced Women's Health

@drsarah_nd

It sounds cliché, but mumma, you really are onboard a hormonal roller coaster from early pregnancy right through your postpartum.

Hormones are amazing – they help create and sustain life, gear your body up for birth and produce your superpower, the ability to supply milk.

But sadly, they don't come without challenges. Hormones cause your body to go through monumental shifts and can affect your skin, your hair, how you sleep, and your emotional and mental health.

That's why it's so important to understand some of the science behind hormones so you can be kind to yourself and access the right support.

So, you have just birthed a beautiful baby. What happens next?

POSTPARTUM AND PERIMENOPAUSE

This is the phase of the rollercoaster where your relaxin, oestrogen, and progesterone head south, while your oxytocin and prolactin levels increase.

> In fact, within 24 hours following birth, your oestrogen and progesterone plummet to perimenopausal levels.

Yes, perimenopausal. You read right. And if you happen to be experiencing both at the same time, you've been cast a double whammy. Be kind to yourself, you're not going crazy. Your body and hormones are in overdrive.

Perimenopause vs Postpartum

Perimenopause

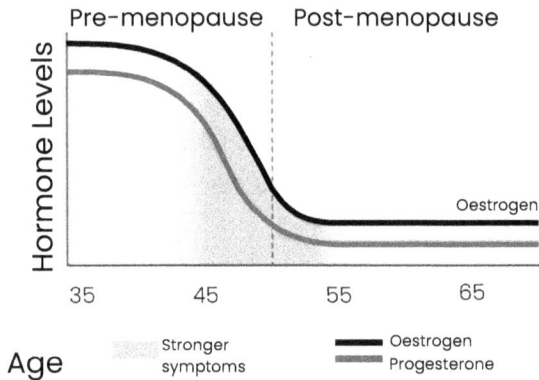

Pre-menopause   Post-menopause

Hormone Levels

Oestrogen

35   45   55   65

Age

Stronger symptoms

Oestrogen
Progesterone

Postpartum

Hormone Levels

Presence of Oestrogen & Pregnancy

Parturition (giving birth)

Progesterone

Oestrogen

1st Trimester   2nd Trimester   3rd Trimester   Postpartum

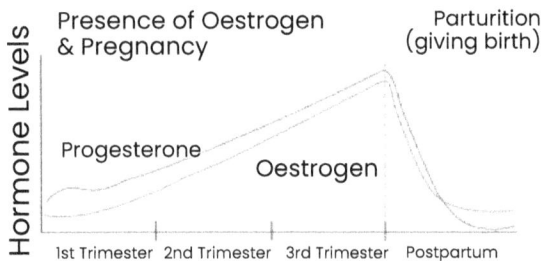

No wonder you're feeling all over the place, just look at how rapidly your key sex hormones plummet after birth, as with perimenopause.

Yes, hormones are a force to be reckoned with. But they're also a double-edged sword as they affect how you feel and how your body responds. Here's a list of some of the things that you can feel and encounter thanks to hormones, with **postpartum women experiencing very similar experiences to that of perimenopausal women:**

- **Immense euphoria or 'baby lust'** (driven by high levels of oxytocin, referred to as "the love hormone")
- **Anxiety, confusion and overwhelm, irritability, anger, rage, baby blues, depression** (this is largely driven by the reduction in progesterone and serotonin which tend to affect mood)
- **Night sweats, skin changes, vaginal dryness, breast tenderness, headaches** (this is largely driven by the reduction in oestrogen levels)
- **"Hair loss"** (low levels of oestrogen increase the rate of hair follicle shedding which is why it may appear that you're 'losing hair' – don't be alarmed, this is only temporary! Seek support from a medical practitioner if you're in any way concerned)
- **Sleep changes and fatigue** (sleep-deprivation goes without saying, and raising a child is stressful! High levels of cortisol, the 'stress hormone,' reduces your melatonin, 'sleep hormone,' and with that, your serotonin, 'feel good hormone,' is reduced, which can easily trigger irritability and frustration i.e. more rest equates to a happier you!)

- **Changes to your libido** (prolactin may inhibit libido - it's Nature's way of saying 'you're busy nurturing your baby, and you have enough on your plate!')
- **Leakage freakage in the bedroom** (aka lactation during sex - if you're breastfeeding, oxytocin, aptly referred to as the 'love hormone,' stimulates the production of prolactin, hence the leakage of milk and wet sheets you may encounter - a real surprise for unexpecting couples!)

Please talk to someone you trust if you're experiencing any of these symptoms and they are interfering with your health and happiness. You don't have to soldier on – there's plenty of support out there.

Wild Beginnings from our Mums

"I had quite a bit of anxiety, probably in my Third Trimester and that carried on through the Fourth Trimester as well. I wasn't expecting to be as angry as much as I was. I didn't even know that that was a perfectly normal reaction to becoming a mum. There was a lot of grief as well that I really wasn't expecting."

— Trina, Wellington, NZ.

"I just remember the overwhelming emotions with everything. Yeah. It's obviously a massive learning curve. Everything you're doing is just for the first time, like, how do I do this?"

— Emma, Auckland, NZ.

"We knew there would be hormonal changes but didn't know much about the details of them and their actual effects (especially in combination with physical changes)."

— MJ and Steve, Auckland, NZ.

WHEN WILL MY PERIOD RETURN?

> Most often, 6-12 months postpartum is a good estimate for when your hormones will return to 'normal' (with oestrogen & progesterone generally returning to pre-pregnancy levels by this stage). However, this isn't the case for everyone. For many, it isn't until a few months after they stop breastfeeding. Once your hormones are 'back to normal,' then your period will return.

- Dr Sarah Wilson, Naturopathic Doctor.

Once your period has returned, your hormones are generally considered 'back to normal.' But your normal may be a 'new normal' for you, as your body has changed in its transition into motherhood.

It is important to note that I'm not referring to the initial heavy postpartum period directly following birth here (whether you experience a vaginal or c-section birth) - this is referred to as lochia and may last anywhere between two to six weeks on average.

Instead, I'm referring to your regular, monthly cycle returning.

You can usually expect Aunt Flo to return from her extended vacation around 6-12 months following birth if you're solely breastfeeding. This is the time when your hormones are likely to be more stable and your oestrogen and progesterone levels, your key reproductive hormones, have returned to their pre-pregnancy levels.

But everyone is different. **The return of your period is largely dependent on how you feed your baby:**

> If you choose to bottle-feed, or do a combination of breastfeeding and bottle feeding, your period may return as soon as five weeks after giving birth.

> If you choose to solely breastfeed, your period may only return a few months after you've weaned your baby.

The reason why how you feed your baby affects your period's return is that prolactin, your superpower hormone responsible for milk production, suppresses the return of oestrogen, and with that ovulation and the return of your period. So, if you're solely breastfeeding, your prolactin levels will be high, largely suppressing your oestrogen levels. As you begin to wean your baby, your prolactin levels will begin to decline, and your oestrogen and progesterone levels will start to increase. With this hormonal shift, your period should generally return a few months following once you've weaned your baby, when your oestrogen and progesterone levels are back to their pre-pregnancy levels.

However, note that this is not always the case for everyone. Our bodies are unique, so your ovulations and periods could return at any stage. If you're ever concerned about your cycle, seek professional support from your doctor as soon as possible.

CAN I FALL PREGNANT WHILE BREASTFEEDING?

Moreover, solely breastfeeding doesn't necessarily prevent ovulation, it *suppresses* it. **So yes, you can fall pregnant even if you're solely breastfeeding – even if your period hasn't yet returned!**

The average ovulation occurs 45 days following birth and doesn't necessarily bring about your period's return at the same time. If you're not wanting to potentially fall pregnant while nursing your young one, ensure you seek professional advice regarding appropriate contraception options for yourself.

Apart from how you feed your baby, **the return of your period can also be affected by too much prolactin:** Thyroid disease, stress, and polycystic ovary syndrome (PCOS) can elevate your prolactin levels.

If your prolactin levels are too high, they can stop your periods completely. This is when you need to speak to a professional – because you need to see if it's something that needs medical treatment or can be managed by diet and lifestyle changes.

POSTPARTUM DEPRESSION (PPD) OR POSTPARTUM THYROIDITIS?

> **Roughly 1 in 10 women experience postpartum hormonal imbalances in their thyroids, commonly referred to as Postpartum Thyroiditis.**

– Dr Sarah Wilson, Naturopathic Doctor.

Unfortunately, around 10% of women will experience Postpartum Thyroiditis, which is an inflammation of the thyroid gland (often coming about during pregnancy changes).

Here's the thing, mumma. A hormonal imbalance in your thyroids can show-up in your body and your moods in a way that's very similar to postpartum depression.

If you're feeling one or more of the following symptoms, please go get checked out by your medical professional:

- Anxiety and depression
- Low sex drive
- Cysts or fibroids
- Weight changes
- Chronic fatigue

You can see why it's easily confused with postpartum depression, right?

Unfortunately some women are misdiagnosed with this much more serious condition. Discuss this with your doctor if you're feeling or experiencing any of the above, as a simple few rounds of blood tests to monitor your thyroid's hormones' levels can distinguish this, so you'll be able to have peace of mind that you're receiving appropriate treatment.

> Generally, it's recommended that if you're still not feeling 'your normal' following approximately four months after birth, seek support from your medical professional to discuss your concerns and symptoms with them.

The key thing to ask yourself is: what's your normal?

And yes, this too can be a grey area now that you've birthed a human being. Maybe you had longer cycles before you were pregnant, or your cycle usually appeared like clockwork every 28 days? If your period doesn't show up in its fairly usual fashion, whatever that may look like, it's always best to discuss it with a medical professional.

How your cycle shows up in your life is a sign of your general health. It's always a good idea to keep track of what Aunt Flo is up to and how it makes you feel – even if we'd rather she stayed on vacation just that little bit longer!

When seeking out support, always ensure the information and advice you attain is of trusted, professional opinion so that you can rest assured knowing that your personalised treatment plan will support your overall postpartum healing.

"POSTPARTUM ENDS WHEN A MOTHER STARTS FEELING LIKE HERSELF AGAIN."

- Wendy Wei Xin Poon

The main hormonal players

A look at the main hormonal players and what they do:

FIRSTLY, RELAXIN

As its name suggests, this hormone looks after loosening the ligaments that hold your pelvic bones together and relaxing your uterine muscle during pregnancy. In doing so, it preps your birth canal for delivery. It could take up to five months after having your baby for your relaxin levels to stabilize, so it is recommended that you don't jump straight back into full exercise-mode. During this time, you're still prone to spraining or overstretching your muscles and jeopardizing your joint health. Take it easy, mumma!.

NEXT UP: OESTROGEN

This key sex hormone plays a leading role in developing the foetus in your uterus. It also boosts the performance of your uterus so that it can respond to oxytocin and enlarges your milk ducts to prepare your breasts for milk production. Oestrogen levels tend to physically affect us, affecting our skin, vaginal lubrication, hair growth, and breast tenderness to name a few.

WHAT ABOUT PROGESTERONE?

Well, this other key sex hormone helps your uterus to relax and supports your immune system to put up with foreign DNA (aka your growing foetus). Progesterone levels tend to emotionally affect us, altering our mood levels. Therefore a dramatic reduction in progesterone following birth often brings about the 'baby blues.'

THERE'S ALSO PROLACTIN

An easy way to remember this is "pro lactation". This 'superpower' hormone is all about prepping your breasts for lactation to nurse your baby. Following birth, your prolactin levels increase to support milk production so you can nurse your baby, following the rise in oxytocin levels. Note that your milk can take up to two weeks to properly come in, so don't be alarmed if your milk production is low soon following the birth of your baby - most importantly, seek out professional advice to guide your decision making in how to best support nourishing your baby and continuously monitor this as you go, straight from the start.

LAST, BUT NOT LEAST, OXYTOCIN

You might know her as the 'love hormone.' This hormone is tasked with stretching your cervix to get it ready for birth plus it stimulates your nipples to produce prolactin, and with this, milk. This hormone drives that strong mothering intuition you'll likely feel after you've birthed bubs. After birth, you'll get a surge of oxytocin and then it will slowly start to exit your system in the coming weeks as it starts to stabilize. Increasing oxytocin levels supports a reduction in your stress levels, promotes an increased bonding with your baby and loved ones, encourages prolactin delivery, and your overall mental wellbeing and happiness. **See "Ways to raise your Oxytocin Levels'" at the end of this chapter.**

There are also many other hormones that work behind the scenes - hormones that are always around, but they change following birth. Let's look at a few more of these:

A CLOSER LOOK INTO CORTISOL

Better known as the 'stress hormone,' after you give birth, your cortisol levels increase. This hormone is handy when you're faced with a real threat, and you need your body to kick into fight or flight mode. In the short-term, having cortisol pumping through your body (hand in hand with adrenalin) is appropriate because it makes us more aware of potential dangers and keeps us alert. If your cortisol levels are too high for too long though, several negative situations can occur: your immunity can suffer, you may not ovulate as you should, and it can leave you feeling worn out. The way to bring your cortisol levels back in line is by resting and doing things you love when you can. Gentle exercise like walking, yoga and stretching helps too. **See "Chapter 5 on Self-care" on page 113.**

MUSING OVER MELATONIN

Melatonin supports our sleep and regulates our circadian rhythms. Following birth, melatonin levels drop in sync with the increased cortisol levels, and overall disruption with the demands that a newborn brings. Disrupted sleep to feed and hold your baby is partially responsible for that dreaded 'mumbrain' and constant tiredness. There are many ways to improve your melatonin levels, for example by reducing screen time before bed, trying to get to bed at the same time and avoiding or limiting alcohol or caffeine (even if you know you're going to wake up soon!). **See "Ways to Improve Sleep" at the end of Chapter 1** - I understand this is such a personal experience, and that it may feel that you're trying everything under the sun, and nothing is working, but know that things WILL improve in time. Never stop seeking out support, you don't need to struggle alone.

SEROTONIN

Serotonin is a natural mood regulator, often referred to as the 'feel good' hormone. It helps us feel happy and calm. Serotonin levels are affected by melatonin levels (affected by rest), so serotonin drops too after birth. Therefore, our mood can feel so out of sync in the Fourth Trimester particularly. Along with the dramatic drop in progesterone, which is also largely responsible for our emotional wellbeing, it's no wonder why you may feel anxious, sad, angry, irritable, and overwhelmed following the arrival of your baby, potentially even experiencing the 'baby blues.'

Studies have proven that eating dark chocolate can increase our serotonin level which boosts our mental health, so don't be afraid to splurge when you've just had a baby, mumma!
(Or ever in my opinion)

As you can see, there is a scientific reason why you feel so out of sorts when you transition into motherhood, so don't be hard on yourself, you truly can blame your hormones!

Share this with other expecting and new mums, let's not undermine the enormity of the effect our hormonal shifts play a part in our physical and emotional wellbeing, and road to postpartum recovery.

Wild Beginnings from our Mums

"Thanks for the great information, Pip. This has been helpful for understanding some of the changes and emotions we have been experiencing."

— Ali, NZ.

"We just wanted to reinforce how useful we found the Being a Parent course. We have been struggling since our baby was born so it really helped us to hear what may be causing us to feel that way and that many others go through similar emotions as well."

— MJ and Steven, Auckland, NZ.

"All good to know before having baby! I should go easy on myself. Thanks, Pip."

— Emma, NZ

15 Ways to raise your Oxytocin Levels

Ways to bond with your baby and increase your happiness

15 WAYS TO RAISE YOUR OXYTOCIN LEVELS

1 GET SOME SUNSHINE AND VIT D

Research shows that oxytocin is directly activated and controlled by Vitamin D which is delivered through sunshine.

2 UP YOUR VIT C INTAKE

Vitamin C is another easy way to optimize and increase your levels of oxytocin.

3 IT 'S TEA TIME !

Research shows that chamomile naturally increases oxytocin and lowers cortisol levels.

4 AROMATHERAPY WITH JASMINE OIL

Aromatherapy with Jasmine Oil can increase levels of oxytocin, improve mood, sex drive and sleep.

5 ADD ANISEED TO SMOOTHIES OR DESSERT

It's been found to increase oxytocin in pregnant women & be effective in reducing symptoms of postpartum depression in new mums.

6 INTERPERSONAL TOUCH

Interpersonal touch quickly increases oxytocin levels in the brain. This also includes kissing, cuddling, hugs, sex, massage and even shaking hands!

7 LOVING - KINDNESS MEDITATION

Loving-kindness meditation, or metta, is a meditation practice designed to enhance feelings of kindness for yourself and others. This can help to overcome trauma by practicing gratitude and focusing on the positives.

8 PET YOUR FURBABY

Research shows that just touching your pets lowers your blood pressure and increases your oxytocin levels.

9 SING AND DANCE

Singing lullabies to your baby may encourage bonding through increasing the release of oxytocin. Dancing has the same effect, so get up and move!

10
YOGA

Yoga is a popular "mind-body" relaxation technique that increases the activity of your parasympathetic "rest and digest" nervous system. Why not try a 'Mums & Bubs' class? This can also help to overcome trauma.

11
VOLUNTEER

Charitable behaviour reduces stress and improves health by increasing oxytocin levels. Plus, it's always good to pay it forward!

12
SOCIALIZE

Talk to people whenever you get the chance, and hang out with your loved ones as much as possible.

13
WATCH A MOVIE

Research shows that compelling narratives cause the synthesis and release of oxytocin.

14
GIVE SOMEONE A GIFT

Studies show that receiving and giving gifts increase oxytocin levels in the brain.

15
DON'T GET HUNGRY!

Eating makes people feel calm and satisfied, and often opens them up for social interaction, bonding and attachment.

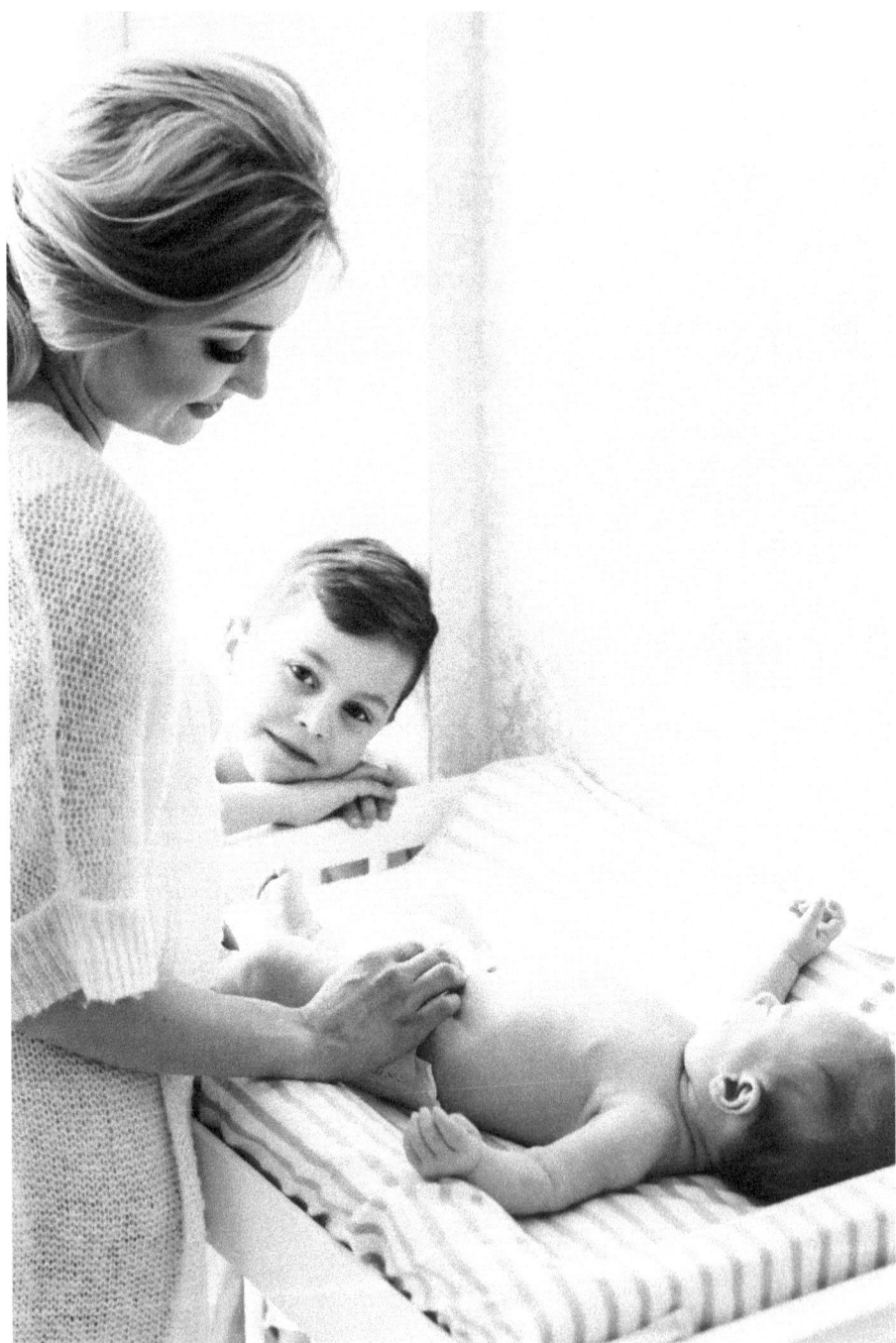

CHAPTER THREE
Confronting unspoken experiences

TACKLING THE TABOO TOPICS OF PARENTHOOD

Confronting unspoken experiences and embracing the wildness

Parenthood is a complex world and every parent's journey is different. Just as we're all different individuals, or like zebras where no stripe is the same, every child is different, and **everyone's parenting style and journey will differ** (even between different children within the same household).

Parenthood also comes with controversial encounters or views that can be tricky to navigate. Being aware of these now can help you steer your feelings and reactions if you're confronted with one of these situations.

There are a lot of topics we could cover here, but I've chosen a few in this chapter that relate to us as parents, and how we can learn to control how we feel about them.

I should also note that **awareness of our own expectations plays a huge role in how we perceive our parenting journey,** and how much pressure we place on ourselves affects our mental wellbeing and experiences. We must try to remember to be kind to ourselves. There's nothing quite like #mumguilt. Yes, mum guilt will always exist. But improved awareness and focusing on realistic self-expectations will go a long way to support us.

Being new parents, we already have a huge responsibility. Quite simply, we don't need the additional pressure of society's views adding to the anxiety and guilt that already comes with being a parent.

Let's jump into it.

Happy Parent, Happy Baby. Right?

Naturally if you have a happy baby, you're going to be a happy parent. Seeing your beautiful baby smile and giggle with delight must make you the happiest parent on the planet. Wrong!

> Let's be honest. Parenting is difficult and you'll have tough days. There'll be moments when you realise it's 2pm and you haven't eaten breakfast yet. You may find yourself crying in the shower or you'll be at your wit's end wondering why your baby won't stop crying.

As a new parent, you're learning to live on more adrenaline. Sleep deprivation shoots up your adrenaline, which increases your cortisol levels i.e. your stress hormones. As adrenaline increases, your sleep hormone melatonin, drops. And your feel-good hormone, serotonin, also drops.

So, you're going to have tough days. **But what is perhaps even tougher is the pressure on us to be happy all the time.** And the idea that if you can put your stress and anxiety aside, the good energy will rub off on your baby.

Of course, your baby is going to feel your emotions. But your baby will also feel if you are trying to put up a façade of being happy.

Instead of trying to distract yourself from what's really going on, try own it and embrace it. Open up, be honest with your baby, and tell them that Mum's having a tough day and that your partner or support person is also finding this tricky.

And it's okay. **Because your baby also has tough days too.** They've just entered this new world and are experiencing incredible developmental leaps. They're experiencing sleep regression. They're encountering different sights, smells, sounds and people. They're feeling the motion of a car, sensing the wind in their face, and smelling what's outdoors.

Their day is also filled with big emotions. Between the two of you, you're going through a lot.

So, let's try and place less pressure on ourselves. Nobody needs the added guilt that comes with parenting.

Cherish the memories and talk to your baby. And when you have moments that feel difficult, ask if someone can help while you take a walk and take some time for yourself.

Your world and your lifestyle have changed. Take it easy. You're doing a **good** job. All you need to do is keep it up and continue to remind yourself that you are one badass mumma!

PARENTAL INSTINCT IS A MYTH

Is parental instinct innate?

Does our parental instinct kick in naturally as soon as we have our baby? Or is that a myth?

> New Zealand journalist, Virginia Fallon, said it best. "Maternal instinct is a myth that endangers mums and babies. Believe it or not motherhood (I would say parenthood) isn't something that comes naturally to women and to me."

– Stuff.co.nz, 15 April 2021.

Society pressures us to believe that maternal and paternal instinct is something that we're born with and that it kicks into gear as soon as we have our baby.

We're led to believe that we're supposed to know how to innately care for babies, as if we're born knowing what to do, but it's not the case. It's an unrealistic expectation that we're setting for ourselves. This expectation can lead a lot of parents into a dark place if they don't feel this 'natural instinct.'

Would you drive a car without lessons?

To prepare for driving a car, you likely would have taken lessons and practised with a family member before you felt confident. You wouldn't have been handed the keys to a car and been instructed to jump onto the motorway and drive from point A to point B if you'd never have been in the driver's seat. **That's basically what parenthood is like. It's suddenly, go for it.**

We must still learn how to become parents ourselves. We must still work through all the different challenges that come with parenting. And that's why you may hear a lot of potentially second- and third-time parents say, "You know, it's actually not that bad." The reason for that is simple - they're no longer as shocked as they were the first time around.

There's nothing quite like the shock that a first-time parent experiences. A second- or third-time parent may feel more experienced in that they can anticipate what to expect (albeit they are now learning how to navigate their older children's and newborn's demands simultaneously, which for them is new too!). It will be okay. You learned how to drive a car or drive a bike, play a musical instrument, talk on the stage in front of others... You catch the drift!) and your confidence will grow with your new-found parenting skills.

So please don't feel pressured into feeling like you should have had some sort of 'natural instinct.' This beautiful new world that you've entered takes time for you all to adapt in as a family.

"The story of the gorilla who learned how to become a mum" on page 74 really resonates with me and highlights that even the natural world enlists the help of its peers. Our village is an incredibly important part of our journey as we learn so much from each other. For example, maternal instinct and breastfeeding are both learned behaviours, so be kind to yourself when you begin to hear that cheeky, little voice in your head starting to mutter away that you "should have this," or that "this is supposed to be easy," or that "this is supposed to come naturally."

Give yourself a break mumma!

THE STORY OF THE GORILLA WHO LEARNED HOW TO BECOME A MUM

The story below, told by the La Leche Leage International, illustrates just how important the observation of breastfeeding really is, indicating that both maternal instinct and breastfeeding truly are learned behaviours:

"In a zoo in Ohio, a female gorilla was born and raised in captivity, got pregnant and had a baby gorilla. On the day she had her baby, she didn't know what to do. She had never seen another gorilla nurse, and she had no concept of breastfeeding. Sadly, the baby gorilla died.

When she became pregnant again the gorilla's keeper called the local La Leche League and had volunteer nursing moms come down to the zoo and nurse their own babies in front of the pregnant momma gorilla. At first the gorilla ignored them, but as her delivery date grew closer she became very interested. When the baby gorilla was born the momma gorilla forgot all that she'd learned and started to freak out. The keeper quickly called the La Leche League and another volunteer rushed over and slowly showed the momma gorilla what to do.

She brought her baby's chest to her chest, slowly cradled the baby's head in her left arm, held her breast with her right hand, and tickled the baby's lips with the nipple to get the baby to open his mouth. Then she pulled the open-mouthed baby toward her breast and with one rapid arm motion, got the cooperative baby quickly onto her breast. The gorilla watched, mimicking the moves step by step until, with a nearly audible sigh of relief, the gorilla looked down at her chest and saw her baby feeding happily for the first time. We are no different - breastfeeding is a skill, and sometimes it just helps to watch another mom breastfeed."

- La Leche Leage International

Bonding can take time

LOVE AT FIRST SIGHT. OR NOT?

Roughly 20% of women say they don't automatically bond with their babies following birth. It's something we shy away from talking about, but there are scientific reasons for this, and they play a much bigger role than you might think.

Commonly referred to as the 'love hormone,' oxytocin provides that strong mothering pull and intuition you'll likely feel following birth ('babylust'). But don't be alarmed if you don't!

> **On average, 1 in 5 women don't feel an immediate connection with their baby directly after birth.**
>
> **– Dr Sarah Wilson, Naturopathic Doctor.**

You've probably dreamt of this moment for a long time, finally getting to meet your baby. Maybe ever since you peed on a stick and found out you were pregnant. Maybe even before that when you started thinking about having a family of your own.

You'd imagined that you'd set eyes on your baby and instantly fall in love.

It's perfectly normal to expect and crave the automatic euphoria when you first set eyes on your baby. That's what oxytocin is meant to do, right?

But sadly, there's no guarantees for new mums and instant bonding doesn't automatically occur. It can feel incredibly disappointing when it's not the love at first sight you'd envisioned.

Please don't beat yourself up if you don't instantly fall in love with your baby, it doesn't make you any less of a mum.

Giving birth is one of the most profound life experiences you will ever encounter, so when your baby is placed in your arms, it's okay if you don't have an immediate and insatiable euphoria. Your mind is still trying to come to terms with what has just happened – you have just brought another living being into this world, who is fully dependent on you for survival – while your body is in full recovery-mode, with great hormonal shifts taking place.

Your hormones alter following birth and once the placenta is delivered. You've got huge, huge shifts happening, and so because your body is naturally all over the place, how you're feeling is all over the place too.

Sometimes, we don't feel like we've truly bonded with baby until they first smile at us or interact with us in another way. **Some relationships take time and you've got a lifetime ahead of you to create gorgeous moments.** Your birth moment isn't your one and only shot at this. Your birth doesn't define your and your baby's happily ever after. And remember, every birth is different.

Try not to compare yourself to other mums or even your dream scenario.

I've noticed the shame and embarrassment that can come from mums who don't feel that instant bond. It's important to see this as a common experience – remind yourself that 20% of women don't feel that instant connection with their baby – YOU ARE NOT ALONE, and YOU ARE NOT THE REASON FOR THIS.

In the Fourth Trimester, difficulties with feeding, traumatic birth experiences, health issues, and sleep deprivation can all impact your relationship with your baby, just to name a few. It's important to be kind to yourself and acknowledge what you've been through, and are still going through.

I want you also to remind yourself that your hormones are all over the place. From the moment your placenta is delivered following birth, you are on a rollercoaster of emotions and hormones. Be super kind and gentle to yourself as you navigate this and don't be afraid to ask for as much help and support as you need.

Skin-to-skin, baby massage, talking to your baby, and being able to do at least one small thing for yourself a day can all help with bonding. **See "15 Ways to raise your Oxytocin Levels" on page 63 and "15 ways to bond with your baby" at the end of this chapter.** Carve out just ten minutes each day to sit quietly if you can or go for a walk with baby, as this can change your perspective and help reduce feelings of resentment or overwhelm.

Don't worry if you don't feel like you're overflowing with love and it doesn't feel natural, you can take baby steps (excuse the pun!) to grow your relationship. And the love will come, oh it will.

Wild Beginnings from our Mums

"I had awful trouble with bonding for a long time and I just quietly opened up to one of the other mums, and she said, 'Oh, you know, I'm going through the same thing as well.' But that took a while to be able to a) know what it was and then b) be able to share outside of just me and my husband and my sister what was actually going on.

For both of us (mum and baby), the bonding issues have improved over time. There are still sometimes it's not where I'd like it to be. I remember saying to my husband, 'It's really weird because during the day I feel like I'm babysitting your child and then when you come home from work you take over, but I stop being a mum.' Like, it becomes your daughter after that. I just happen to be her carer.

It's a really weird sensation, but I guess the normalising helped me to get out and have one on one catch-ups with mums that were affected, which I probably wouldn't have done before. Things have definitely started to improve in time, and when she started smiling and giving back to me, I felt that that's when our bonding really started to take form."

— From Trina, Wellington, NZ.

"The first 16wks are intense and it takes time to feel a deep connection with your baby - like any relationship, it takes time to get to know your baby, but you'll quickly get to know them and the deep love will follow - remember, you're doing the most important job in the world in a sleep deprived state with a huge amount of postpartum hormones in your system mucking with your emotions. Just keep your values front and centre rather than "how well" you think you're doing."

— From Lydia, Auckland, NZ.

"I struggled with the initial bond with my daughter, Ella, which made me feel terrible but my midwife reminded me that this is normal and there is nothing 'wrong with me,' so I think it's important for people to know this can happen and there is nothing wrong with you when this happens! The bond does happen, it can just take time."

- Sarah, NZ.

"You've got to accept that you're a beginner again - that's probably one of the hardest things."

- Emma, Auckland, NZ

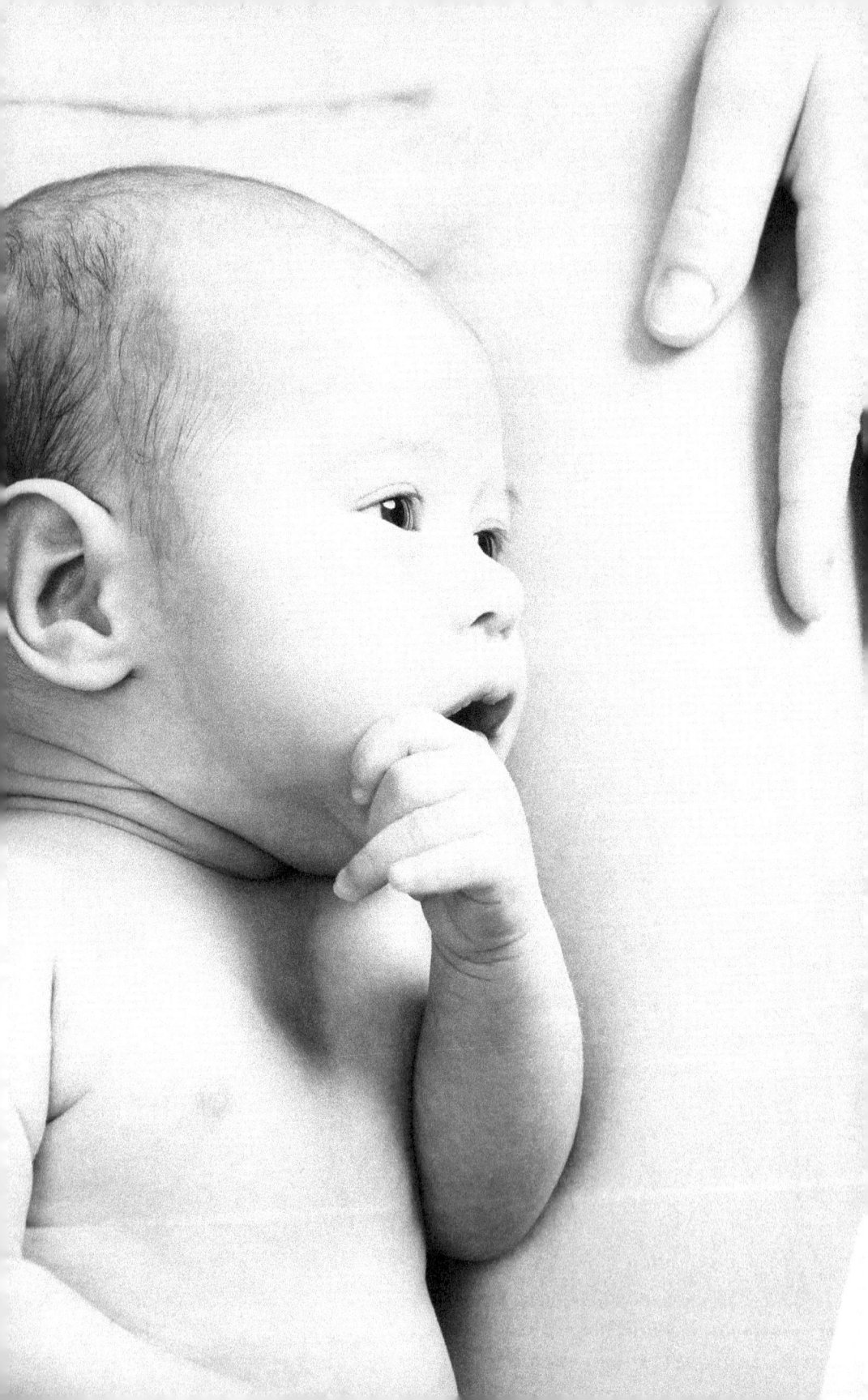

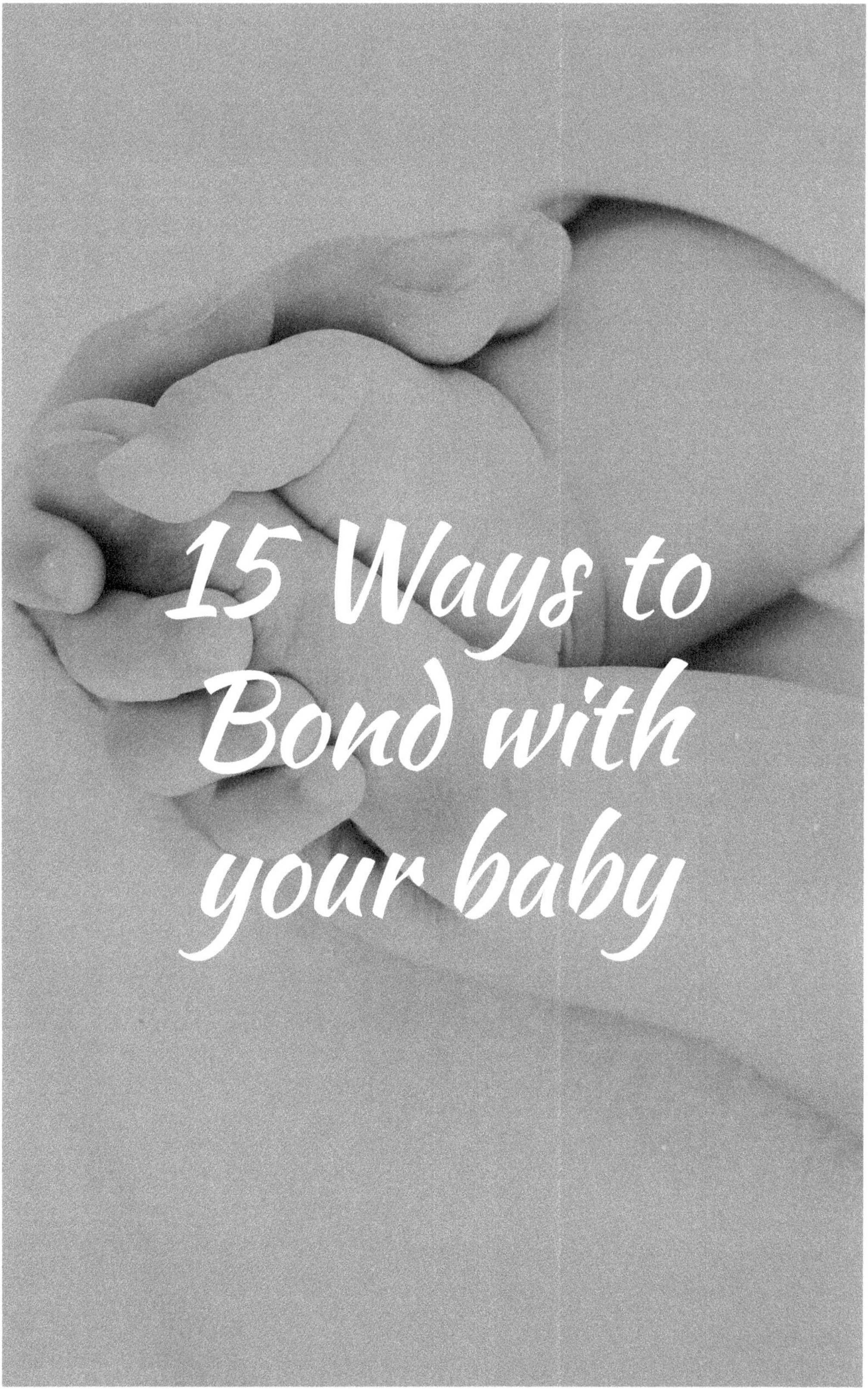
15 Ways to
Bond with
your baby

15 WAYS TO BOND WITH YOUR BABY

1

SKIN-TO-SKIN CONTACT

Hold your baby against your skin, promoting closeness and comfort.

2

EYE CONTACT

Gaze into your baby's eyes while feeding or cuddling, or while lying on the floor together. Try to look at things through your baby's eyes to gain a new perspective, talk to your bubs.

3

CUDDLING AND SNUGGLING

Hold your baby close, providing warmth and comfort.

4

BABY MASSAGE

Gently massage your baby's body using baby-safe oils. Google local classes that offer this, it's a great way to connect with other mums at a similar stage as you.

5

NOURISHING YOUR BABY

Feeding time fosters a strong connection, breast- or bottle-feeding.

6

BABYWEARING AND DANCING

Carry your baby in a sling or carrier while going about your day; or have fun dancing around the house with bubs – in or out of carrier; there are even babywearing dance classes you can attend. Enjoy being playful and silly together, it's just the two of you having fun!

7

SINGING AND TALKING

Your voice is soothing and helps your baby recognize you.

8

READING OUT LOUD

Even newborns enjoy hearing your voice while you read, is there a favourite story from your childhood you loved to hear that you can read to your little one and relive those wonderful memories?

9

PLAYTIME

Use age-appropriate toys and engage in simple games.

10

TUMMY TIME

Place your baby on their tummy while awake to encourage interaction; having baby lie against you on your tummy counts as well!

11

BATHING

Bond during bath time by talking, smiling, and splashing gently.

12

EXPLORATION

Introduce your baby to new sights, sounds, smells and textures.

13

GO FOR WALKS, VISIT NEW PLACES TOGETHER

Stroll outdoors and enjoy the sights, sounds, and fresh air. Go somewhere you've always wanted to, but never planned before. On this day, plan that you have no other errands and try time the outing for as soon as bubs has woken from his/ her first morning nap. Be brave, step out of your comfort zone with bubs – together you are allies in your new encounter.

14

BABY'S INTERESTS

Pay attention to what your baby likes and respond to their cues.

15

BE PRESENT

Spend uninterrupted time together, minimizing distractions. Don't feel guilty about the amount of time you get to spend with baby – quality time over quantity, always!

Remember, bonding is a unique journey, and finding what works best for you and your baby is key. Try not to worry about the amount of time it takes for your bond to develop, it will continue to strengthen over time.

"IN THE AGE OF SOCIAL MEDIA, WHEN YOU CAN EDIT YOUR LIFE IN BEAUTIFUL PICTURES, IT'S IMPORTANT TO REMIND MOMS THAT ALL OF US ARE WEARING YOGHURT AND ALL OF OUR HANDS SMELL LIKE URINE."

– Kristen Bell, Actress

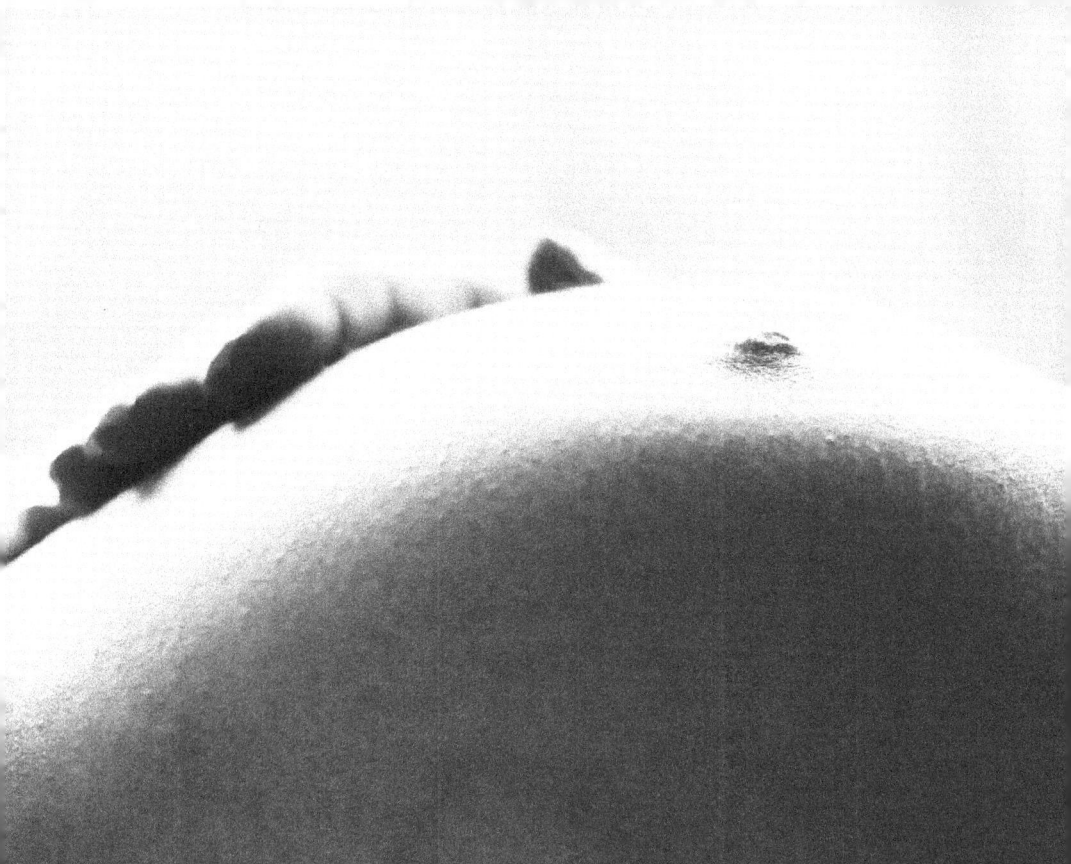

CHAPTER
FOUR
Your Matrescence

ENTERING YOUR MATRESCENCE IN THE FOURTH TRIMESTER

Transitioning into Motherhood
The Tug-of-war Effect

> **We know that it's normal for teenagers to feel all over the place. So why don't we talk about pregnancy in the same way?**

- Dr Alexandra Sacks

Reproductive Psychiatrist, Author & TED Presenter

@alexandrasacksmd

Watch TED talk here

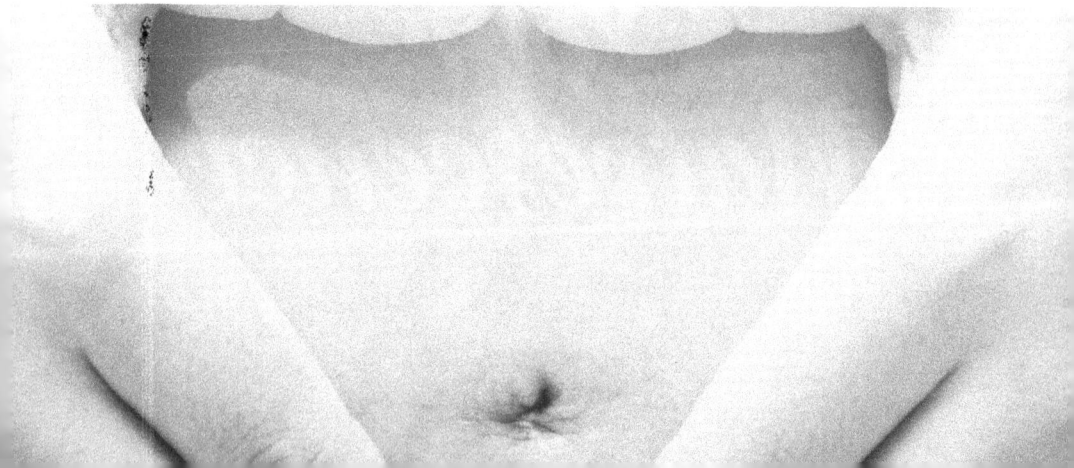

Becoming a parent may have you feeling a raft of emotions, 'I'm not good at this. I thought I'd always want to put the baby first. Is there something wrong with me? Do I have postpartum depression?'

What's highlighted here is that you've set yourself up for parenthood with unrealistic expectations.

One of my favourite quotes from Dr Alexandra Sacks, a reproductive psychiatrist, best-selling author and TED presenter, is, **'Discomfort is not always the same as disease'.** This leads us to Matrescence.

The Tug-of-war: The Pull vs Push

The Anthropologist, Dana Raphael, defined matrescence as the transition from woman to mother in her book "Being Female: Reproduction, Power and Change," in 1973. Matrescence is the transition to motherhood, and it comes with an emotional tug-of-war effect, or as Dr Alexandra Sacks refers to it, as the pull-and-push effect.

Why do teenagers feel all over the place? They're undergoing adolescence, a monumental physical and hormonal change. It's no surprise then that matrescence is similar to adolescence. This is the phase of our lives where we're transitioning into the new world of motherhood, and yet again, encountering a monumental physical and hormonal change at this next stage of our reproductive lifecycle.

Yet, unlike adolescence, matrescence isn't openly spoken about in society.

When we experience substantial physical and hormonal changes simultaneously, this will result in us feeling different emotionally.

The pull side of this tug-of-war of matrescence is the hormonal, physiological pull that comes with being a parent which propels you to care for and nurture your newborn. Oxytocin, referred to as the 'love hormone,' is released around childbirth and through skin-to-skin touch.

The other side of the rope is the push effect, your mind pushing you away from wanting to be the responsible caregiver. This is your brain telling you, 'Remember what it used to be like when I didn't have a baby.' 'Remember when I could just up and walk out and didn't have this accessory attached to me 24/7.'

Your brain reminds you that you have other aspects to your life: the need for your own physical space, relationships, work, hobbies, exercise and more.

The pull- and push- effects bring about a real emotional tension, the #mumguilt that we know all too well. **There's the pull of wanting to give your all to your baby, but there's the push of wanting to have your own space and time as well.**

Sometimes it can feel like it's hard to win the tug-of-war, as if the rope is constantly being pulled back-and-forth the winning mark. Learning to embrace this constant tension is the epitome of matrescence, and understanding that this is a normal, universal experience, allows for a smoother transition into the wild world of parenthood.

Getting to know the new you.

The transition to motherhood often brings new mums to question who they are as individuals, outside of 'just a mum.' Often new mums state that they grieve for the person they used to be and identify a sense of feeling invisible as majority of the attention is now on the baby.

This is all very normal, and if you too feel like this, you are not alone.

It's absolutely normal to miss your career, social life, your fitness routine, your date nights with your partner, and more.

Don't push your feelings away or try to numb them. It's okay to acknowledge them. Open up and talk to other mums around you and you'll be surprised how many of them feel the same way. Remember, this is just the part of being on the 'push' side of the tug-of-war of your matrescence.

Our thoughts appear to contradict each other, and we're often left feeling anxious, confused, and overwhelmed in the tension that the tug-of-war of matrescence brings with it.

Your life has turned upside down in a matter of moments once your baby has arrived, and you're learning and adjusting to new experiences, routines and in the process, focusing on healing and rebuilding yourself. There are several forces at play here, so feeling uneasy in your new lifestyle, and potentially questioning what the future holds, is completely understandable.

But having a baby is also your chance to reinvent yourself, take stock of what you value, and bring things back into your life that bring you happiness and light you up.

> **Dr Alexandra Sacks highlights that, "When you preserve a separate part of your identity, you're also leaving room for your child to develop their own."**

– Dr. Alexandra Sacks, Reproductive Psychiatrist.

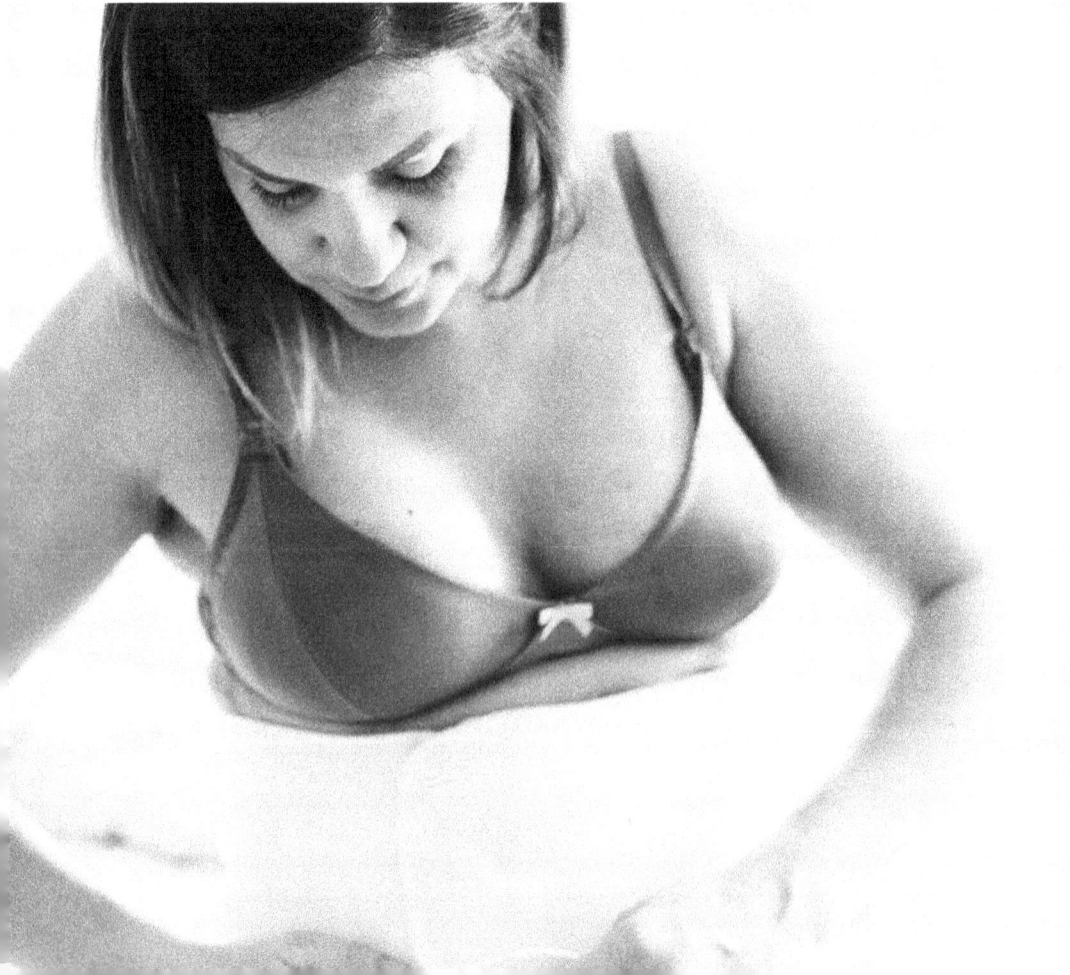

Ask yourself

*W*hat's important to me?

*W*hat do I value?

*W*hat do I want for myself and my family?

Having a baby doesn't mean you have to sacrifice every part of you that you loved before you had your baby. You're still in there – even if your hormones try to convince you otherwise.

Self-care and finding what brings you joy is very important as a new mum, and it doesn't have to be elaborate or expensive. Find a pocket of peace today or tomorrow to take some time out to ask yourself – what can I do in the next day, week, or month to show myself some self-love and get to know and appreciate the new me? **See "Self-care" on page 113 and "A plan to thrive" on page 181.**

You are a mum, yes. But you're more than that too and you can get to love the new you. Take your time and don't put any pressure on yourself to feel or be a certain way.

Wild Beginnings from our Mums

"There was a lot of grief that I really, really wasn't expecting. Another friend described it as you've got an emotional tank and different things fill it up, and you get to a certain point where you can't fit anymore in your tank. And I wasn't getting the self-care that I needed to kind of deplete that tank a little bit to allow room for it to be refilled by her screaming, day after day. So, I was just flipping my lid all the time."

— Trina, Wellington, NZ.

"As soon as you have the baby, it's like you're invisible. Everyone addresses the baby and talks to them, and you feel like you've been hit by a train. My advice is to put your mental health and your baby's health first. But yeah, you've got to make sure that you are ready to face some huge challenges and changes and look after yourself in the process as well. And it takes a village."

— Annalise, Dunedin, NZ.

THE MOTHERHOOD ICEBERG

Embracing emotional and relationship changes: the challenges and the beauty

In parenthood, you're navigating a new world. A lot can change in your relationships — between you and your partner, with your family, and with your friends and colleagues.

I like to use the iceberg analogy to describe parenthood and look at the layers beneath the surface, to demonstrate what you may be experiencing versus what you're seeing, or believe you're witnessing, on the outside. It's easy to fall victim to the comparison game!

There are incredible moments that come with being a parent, but due to the complexity of the world of parenthood, there are particularly challenging times too.

I get wonderful feedback and stories from sharing the iceberg analogy in my live workshops as parents share their experiences with each other.

> Sharing and speaking up is the key here. In silence we feel as if we're the only ones living these experiences, but when you share with other parents, you realise everyone is dealing with similar things. You are not alone, ever. We'll soon take a look at what some of these experiences and feelings look like.

Speak up – in your own way!

It can feel unnerving to voice your feelings. And sometimes it takes a while to get there. **Start with a form of communication that's comfortable for you.** I started a gratitude journal and wrote down what I was grateful for during difficult times, so that I could gain perspective and start to balance the tough moments with the great times.

People ask me when I found the time to sit and write, but the majority of my journaling was on the notes app in my phone! Just getting these thoughts out of your system is key. You may prefer to jot down your notes, express yourself on post-it notes, or there are a range of journaling apps to suit you.

Journaling really does help and has been proven to reduce stress levels and negative thoughts, even improving immunity levels for some!

Speaking up and seeking help can also be done through free Healthline or counselling services. Sometimes we just need an ear to lean on as it can be hard to express our deepest thoughts and feelings with those closest to us. A parents' coffee group can be especially helpful, or if you feel comfortable expressing to your partner, family and friends, by all means do. **The key is to talk about your thoughts that are consuming your mind.**

The rollercoaster of parenting

Parenting is a wild ride. It's packed with incredible moments that far outweigh the many difficult moments. It's incredible to watch your mini-me learn from you and grow up right in front of you.

Yet, the expectations we place on ourselves and the feeling that we're not meeting them can make our stomach queasy. Before we became parents, we may have thought we were going to strive to be the 'perfect' parents or do all the 'right' things.

> We need to embrace imperfections. We are ourselves not perfect, so how can we expect our parenting to be perfect? How can we expect our children to be perfect when they're not going to be perfect? Imperfection is beautiful, the world doesn't want or need cookie-cutter versions of everything. Instead of striving for perfection, why not focus more on embracing imperfection?

THE MOTHERHOOD ICEBERG

Here are several scenarios that parents in my workshops have opened up about. I hope you find comfort in realising you are not alone if they resonate with you.

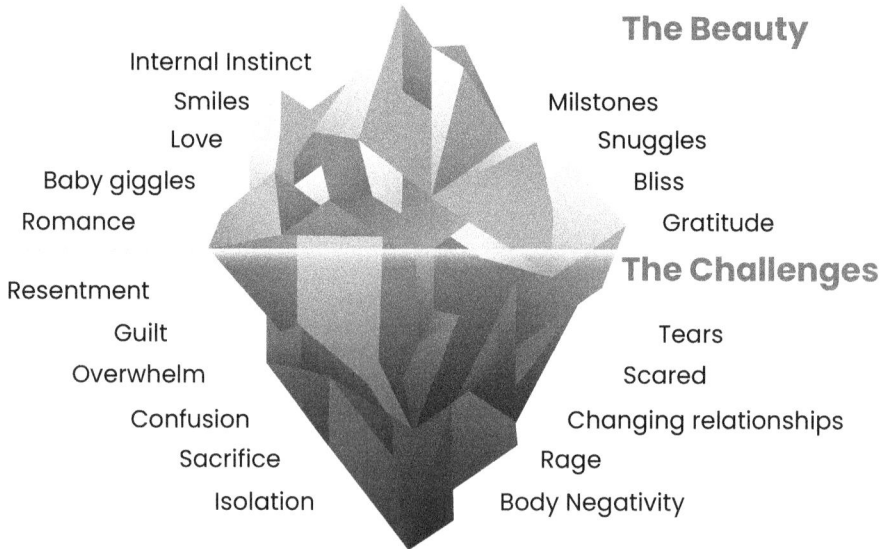

The Beauty

Internal Instinct
Smiles
Love
Baby giggles
Romance
Milstones
Snuggles
Bliss
Gratitude

The Challenges

Resentment
Guilt
Overwhelm
Confusion
Sacrifice
Isolation
Tears
Scared
Changing relationships
Rage
Body Negativity

UNDERNEATH THE SURFACE
THE CHALLENGES:

Resentment

With an imbalance in recovery and responsibilities that becoming a parent brings with it, it's common for new parents to experience resentment towards each other from time to time. Communication between partners is key. To avoid the build-up of resentment, clearly communicate your needs with your partner, and **try to remember that they are not mind-readers** (as much as we would love them to be!). Perhaps you could suggest saying to your partner, "I'm feeling so exhausted and sore, it's hard for me to focus on anything but feeding the baby right now. It would be so helpful for me if you could (xyz)…" **This can help you both share the load of new parenthood.**

Grief

Grieving the 'old' you is a very real feeling. Acceptance of a very different lifestyle compared to that of one prior to having children is a serious adjustment, and the realisation that it's a permanent shift can be unsettling to start with, especially in a sleep-deprived state! Your new world revolves around your baby, your home, new routines, and experiencing clear "wins" within the day can appear few and far between (apart from potentially smooth transfers of baby into the bassinet – a real win I might add!).

While you may find yourself contemplating, 'Now I'm just a mum.' There's no 'just' here. You're an incredible parent, and you're doing a phenomenal job. The 'before' you still exists, and she's around the corner waiting for you. **Right now, you're just knee-deep in the world of navigating life with a newborn.** Know that soon you'll emerge from the depths of early motherhood and find joy in growing with and creating incredible memories alongside your little one, who will learn more and more from you in every passing day. **See "Getting to know the new you." on page 91 in Chapter 4, Your Matrescence.**

If you feel you aren't coping, and this sinking feeling does not seem to move on, please seek help. There are medical professionals who specifically focus on supporting new parents who experience this, and you are not alone. **Your emotions are valid.**

"I'M NERVOUS ABOUT THE NEW ME - PHYSICALLY AND MENTALLY."

– Hannah, NZ.

Guilt

For every one thing you do, there's another thing you could have done, and you're constantly weighing up each option. Sometimes you struggle to make decisions and other times you may feel as if you made the wrong one.

There's so much to parenting. It consists of multiple 'little windows', especially in the first couple of years. Think of these things as a window that will pass. These are the first few months of your baby's life, and your baby will grow up to be an incredible human being – no matter how you feed your baby, no matter how your baby sleeps, and no matter what routines you do or don't follow with your baby – so stop beating yourself up!

Overwhelm

One of the most used words to describe early parenthood, is 'overwhelm.' You're thrown into a new world, and the confusion and changes that come with it.

Many parents I've spoken with feel they weren't prepared when the birth happened. They still had a list of things to do and since their baby arrived, they're playing catch up. Along with the never-ending list of tasks on their plates, there's the unpredictable nature of newborns, the unsolicited (and often contradictory!) advice, and a bombardment of opinions thrown their way.

When feeling overwhelmed or stressed out, raise your hand and ask for help. Also, try not to fester on the thought that this may just be you dealing with this experience, as while many mums may be describing this "as the most magical period of their lives," which could cause you to question whether you're 'doing things right or not,' they may just be less outspoken than you about the various challenges they're experiencing.

Our motherhood experiences are unique to us, our babies are unique, but what is not unique is the wild ride we're all on! Don't lose sight of this, and if it helps, envision the iceberg when you find yourself comparing yourself to others who you believe are coping better than yourself, we never quite know what's happening beneath the surface. You aren't alone, and there is help for you**. See Chapter 5 "Self-care" on page 113**, and read up on how to create windows of peace amongst the wildness.

Sacrifice

This often goes together with 'grief'. It can come into play when parents don't have their own family or key support network nearby. You may have made the sacrifice to raise a child in a different city or country, or you may feel as if you've sacrificed the person you were before to become a parent, and that element of your previous life has disappeared.

In times like this, **remind yourself that it's important to preserve a part of yourself,** to find something that you love doing outside of 'just being a mum,' and to go out and do it. It could be as simple as managing a walk with a hot coffee in the sunshine alone (while someone you trust looks after your baby of course). **Preserving a part of your identity will encourage your child to feel safe in identifying their own identity, independently.**

Isolation

You may feel alone without family support. This could be due to physical or emotional distance. Or it could be a feeling of being alone in your experiences, that you're 'the only one' not coping with certain challenges of parenthood. I absolutely encourage you to seek help if this resonates with you.

If you don't feel comfortable speaking up about how you are feeling, perhaps start with expressing yourself and experiences through journaling. **Writing things down helps to remove the thoughts that are consuming you, slowly unravelling the power away from these negative emotions,** and this can help bring about a new perspective. When you're ready, I encourage you to share with someone you trust and feel comfortable around, or to seek help from a professional. Your emotions are worthy, and you don't need to struggle through things alone. **See the list of resources at the end of this book to learn more about where to find trusted, professional support.**

Body negativity

You've been through massive physical changes, and you need to be kind to this new body of yours. After all, it has completed the magnificent job of growing and birthing a human.

Societal expectations of 'bouncing back' into shape are both physically and emotionally draining. Adopt this new body of yours and be kind to it. It will take a fair amount of time to recover. That's why the postpartum recovery phase is so important. Are you seeking help? Are you feeling good enough about yourself to engage in activities that can help support you? This is your body. And it has done amazing things. So be proud and wear those scars with pride.

However, if you find yourself not being able to come to terms with the physically 'new you,' or things don't appear to get back to your pre-pregnancy normal, discuss your concerns with your doctor and I also suggest you visit a pelvic floor therapist for a postnatal WOF (warrant of fitness) - **See Chapter 8 "Pelvic Health and Exercise" on page 165** to learn more about this.

Rage

Majority of parents don't talk about rage and their intrusive thoughts, but this is a very real and valid emotion.

Pent up exhaustion can bring about rage. It's okay to recognise this, and you should find comfort in knowing that you aren't alone, that every parent experiences this. The key is awareness, to be able to identify this emotion bubbling up before you act on anything. When noticing this feeling surfacing, ensure baby is in a safe space, and step away into another room for a few deep breaths if you need.
If you're with someone you trust, ask if you can step outside for some fresh air while they look after baby.

Make sure that you're getting the help and speaking up about it. Don't feel fearful about talking up, awareness and seeking support are key to improving your situation and overall lifestyle for your whole family.

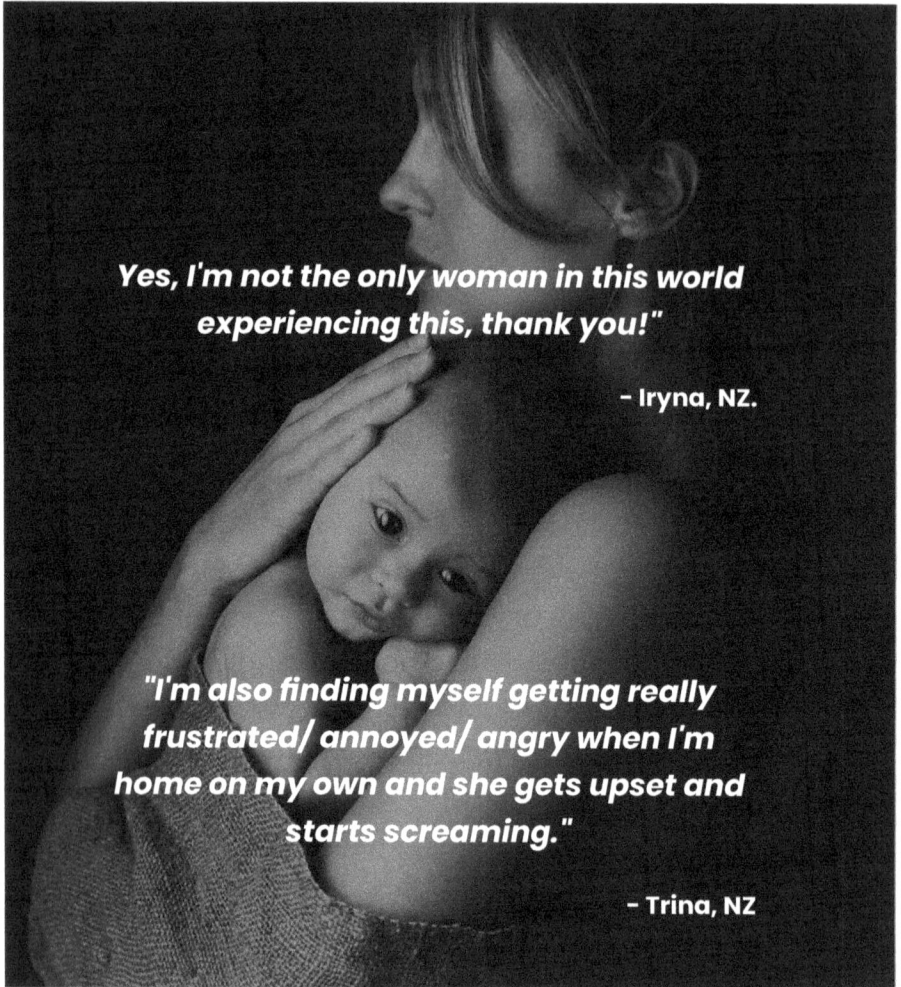

Yes, I'm not the only woman in this world experiencing this, thank you!"

– Iryna, NZ.

"I'm also finding myself getting really frustrated/ annoyed/ angry when I'm home on my own and she gets upset and starts screaming."

– Trina, NZ

Changing relationships

Changing relationships come into play with your partner, family, with friends (with and without children), and with external parties such as colleagues and acquaintances.

Your views affect relationships because your values are front and centre and tied in with your baby's welfare.

Sometimes you can treat things people say like water off a duck's back, but often comments passed from loved ones can affect how you feel about things and cause you to question your parenting abilities, knocking your confidence.

Tension can generally be relieved between yourself and others by listening to others' viewpoints, while explaining your own. At the end of the day, no one knows your baby better than yourself and your partner, so remember to high-five yourself in times of doubt. You DO have this, even when you feel questioned by others.

Scared

One day you're out wining and dining with your friends, and the next, you're responsible for this fully dependent baby. Of course, there is anxiety that comes with this - worrying about the day that your baby will first catch a cold, or if they'll end up in the emergency department one day.

Worrying is completely normal, it shows you're an incredibly, caring parent. **Just be aware of the level of your anxiety,** and if you're not feeling like yourself, then seek help. Only you will be able to judge whether the anxiety is taking over your life and preventing you from experiencing joy with your baby.

"WHEN A CHILD IS BORN,
SO IS THE MOTHER."

Tears

We've all been there; we've shed many tears during both happy and challenging times. It's all about letting go and fully welcoming your emotions. Let. It. Out. Journaling can be helpful in times like this, as is talking with loved ones, getting outside, and having some 'me time.'

I hope that you feel a little bit of relief knowing that these are some of the challenges that EVERY parent has felt. And, and if you continue to experience these things, which you will, then **it's okay just to take a step back and remind yourself, 'Others have felt this way, I'm human and it's NORMAL.'**

However, if at any stage you're not feeling like things are improving and that the challenges are greater than the joy that comes with being a parent, then I implore you to seek help. It's not worth struggling through this on your own, mumma. This should be the most empowering period of your life, so raise your hand, and seek the help you so deserve.

And by raising your hand, you may just encourage other parents to raise their hands too.

ABOVE THE SURFACE – THE BEAUTY

Our beautiful bundles will bring so much light to our lives. They will teach us so much. This is the beauty that comes with parenting.

Romance

Can you recall that feeling when you first realised that you and your partner would become parents together? And when you created this incredible little being? There will be many moments where you'll both say, 'we actually did this, this was us!' What a phenomenal journey you're on.

Becoming parents can most certainly create closer connections between partners, as you develop a new and different level of connection.

Giggles

When your baby first giggles, it makes ALL the hard work worth it. Every night feed, nappy change and screaming car ride has been worth it. There's no way to really describe the immense love both you and baby feel when you're so connected and the gratification that comes with this.

A giggle is a message from your baby that you're doing an incredible job! When you witness that first smile, first hear laughter from your baby, and see the excitement and glimmer in their eyes, there's just no other feeling on the planet like it. Cherish the explosion of your emotions.

Bond

The bond with you and your child will develop in time. It can feel difficult from time to time, especially if you are one of the approximate 20% of women who find it difficult to immediately bond with their newborn babies. For mummas who have found it difficult to bond with their babies, many have highlighted that once their baby starts to smile, the connection between them grows in leaps and bounds.

Ultimately, you're their parent and your relationship will most certainly grow. **The more love you pour into each other, the stronger your bond will develop.** Leaving room for your own identities to flourish will strengthen this bond too. **See "15 Ways to raise your Oxytocin Levels" on page 64 at the end of chapter 2 and "15 Ways to Bond with your baby" on page 84 at end of chapter 3.**

Maternal Instinct

This is a learned behaviour. But once you feel like you've cracked it, you can trust yourself, and have the confidence to speak up and own your parenting style, then you'll feel like you're on top of the world! It will come with time. **You are forever learning with first time experiences, and confidence develops over time.**

Milestones

When you see your baby achieve their milestones, from rolling over, crawling, walking and their first words, these make all the challenges worth it. **The snuggles, the bliss, the gratitude.** Just a few more reasons why being a parent is so darn cool.

Write about all the positive things that parenting brings you, along with the challenges. Talk openly about these beautiful moments so you don't lose sight of the greatness growing in front of you. It's also so easy to forget about these fleeting joys, so, if possible, write letters to your little one, and share the memories that warm your heart so it too can warm their hearts one day.

You've got this, mumma!

CHAPTER FIVE
Self-care

WINDOWS OF PEACE WITHIN THE WILDNESS

Not losing sight of ME-time

Prioritising yourself
A happier you for a happier family

Hmmm... This is rich coming from me... Someone who seldomly makes time for herself, but is writing about self-care. I partially feel like an imposter, but I'm also sure this is 90% of us as mothers. **We know the true value of self-care, yet we often fail to actually practice it!**

Thankfully, alongside my supportive husband and family, I have an incredible village of mummas around me, who, when they see I'm looking burnt out, remind me that my cup needs a top up, and fast! Embracing the wildness is one thing, but if the lioness fails to find rest and to be able to recuperate from the last chase, how will she ensure the family's next meal is ready on time and keep the wee cries at bay?

There's no way around it, there's no doubt, we all need rest.

Rest is the number one item on my list for self-care, even if it's just 5 minutes alone in the sunshine, drinking my HOT cup of coffee (or an ice-cold Pinot Gris come 6pm!). What is it for YOU? And HOW do we get the opportunity to find time to prioritise ourselves, even if it's just within a window of time during the day?

Building awareness of the need to prioritise ourselves is the first step in making a change. To practice a self-care regimen is to develop a new skill, and a skill is mastered over time. So don't be harsh on yourself, or feel guilty, for not making time for you. Just like finding your maternal voice and instinct, it takes time to build this foundation of awareness and to intricately layer your strategic self-care stepping stones on top of it. So, let's begin by putting this into practice today...

Learning to prioritise yourself, building awareness to set the foundation for self-care:

- **Do you feel overwhelmed?** Take a step back, and ask yourself what is the number one thing that is currently consuming you? Is there someone who can help you with this to relieve the load? Can you express how you're feeling, by means of talking to someone you trust, or by putting pen to paper to digest your thoughts and calm your frazzled nerves?

- **Find yourself needing rest?** Whether it's a 20-minute catnap that will do the trick, or you need to curl into a ball and escape for a few hours, if your body is signalling to you that you need this, then how can you plan to follow this through? Everything else can wait, prioritise your rest, and you'll soon feel rejuvenated to be able to tackle the unpredictable nature of what your cute bundle brings.

- **Feeling sluggish?** Start moving, head outside and smell the roses. Talk a walk. Breathe in, deeply, slowly. Pick up a yoga class, or lie down on your carpet and have a good stretch.

- **Feeling guilty?** Here's one for you mumma, self-care is not selfish. You can, and it's important to, give yourself permission to care for yourself. This does not mean you love your baby any less! If you have no access to childcare, it does make it trickier to carve out time for yourself, but don't feel guilty about it when you do make time. **See "Create your f*cket and funday lists" on page 126 towards the end of this chapter.**

- **Feeling disconnected with your partner?** Openly talk to each other, make time for each other at the end of the day. Could you incorporate day-dates? Restore your sense of humour, dance together as a family, be silly. Play. Make a rule, no phones during meals?

- **Feeling disconnected with yourself?** Now's a great opportunity to try something new you've always wanted to try. Create a fun challenge, for example taking black and white photos of something meaningful to you for 7 days, or cooking a new meal every Wednesday, or planting a vege garden, or creating a journal to write letters to your child, or volunteering, the list is endless... Connect with your values, what are they, are you living them? Honour yourself and your feelings.

- **Find yourself playing the comparison game?** Remember that everyone experiences different challenges at different stages, and self-care itself looks, and is, different for everyone. Focus on what brings you joy, and when you genuinely live this, everyone around you, including yourself, will bathe in true happiness. Self-care doesn't have to cost anything either, search for gratitude in the little things (for me, it's sleep, fresh air, sunshine, coffee, wine, chocolate, good music, and snuggles in my pjs with my kids).

- **Or are you just "hangry"?** If it's been too long since you last thought about feeding yourself, or you find yourself being able to barely chew your meals these days, then focus on finding a time when you CAN sit down and enjoy your meal. And always be snack-ready: pack snacks in the car, in the nappy bag, in your lounge, on your bedside table… Could this be a job to delegate to your partner?

Once you've connected with your core feelings, you can begin to strategically layer your self-care stepping stones one on top of the other over time, by concentrating on the following:

- **Honour the power of one** - try to think of doing just one thing for yourself each day. By only focusing on one thing, this helps to reduce the overwhelm. **See chapter 9 "A plan to thrive" on page 181 to support you with this.**
- **Plan to succeed, build your weekly personalised self-care tracker** that you can paste in your wardrobe so you don't lose sight of caring for yourself.
- **Share your self-care journey with others**. You may find they become empowered to follow you in your self-care discovery, and having a self-care buddy can help yourselves remain encouraged and accountable towards your personal self-care regimens. Share more love, share more happiness!
- **Focus on your emotional, social, and physical self-care** to maintain a sense of overall wellbeing.
- **Role model self-care to your children** and watch them build emotional resilience and grow in confidence, developing their own identities and independence.
- **Whenever you feel you're struggling, know that you're not alone.** Share your challenges with your loved ones or involve a professional. It's good to

be vulnerable, again we can role model this to our children. You deserve to feel supported, understood, and empowered.

- **Remind yourself that by unwinding, you can focus on being present with your little one** in this special time. Time really does pass you by, there's no need to rush your day, weeks, months away. You'll blink, and it will be their first birthday...

- **Know that you are one badass mumma**, worthy of self-care!

- **And as always, enjoy being enveloped in the wildness of motherhood!**

Soon you'll well be on your way to including self-care as part of your daily ritual, finding joy in the small things, and leading a more fulfilled, happier life with your little one learning and soaking it all in beside you.

AN ENTREPRENEURIAL MUMMA'S MANTRA & HER TOP 20 TIPS

Charlotte, kiwi mumma of Esme and Roman, is a good friend of mine, and the talented family photographer behind Olive and Pop. She is also a motherhood and lifestyle blogger, and is an absolute expert at capturing the soulful essence of motherhood through her creativity in both her photography, and writing. Running a business, and running a household, intertwines the busyness of life to the point that it can feel almost impossible to escape the chaos and overwhelm, but over the years Charlotte has developed some fantastic self-care strategies to ensure she doesn't let her cup run dry, or her enthusiasm for her life and family dissipate.

This is Charlotte's story, and her Top 20 Tips for staying ahead of the overwhelm game:

*Self-care is one of the most important aspects of my life. It is the ultimate way for me to live my life with my children, Esme and Roman, according to our family values. I love this life we have with every ounce of my being and **I don't want the busyness to encroach on the simple moments of this extraordinary, ordinary life together.***

-Charlotte Clements, mumma of Esme and Roman, Christchurch, NZ.

WILDBEGINNINGS.THINKIFIC.COM | PIP FINDLAY

So for me, caring for myself is enabling the kind of mothering I want to embody and to be the best mumma I can be to model this and to show up as the most vibrant and integrated person. I practise self-care because I have an awareness of the immensity of raising the next generation. These children have entrusted us with their care and gifted us with the opportunity for growth, expansion, so I want to do the best I can for them. That means taking care of myself first in the most holistic way.

Self-care can differ from person to person and once someone has tapped into their intuition or soul desire, their awareness of their life philosophy or values will reveal with so much clarity. *But to me, self-care is joy, mindfulness, connection to each other and to my soul - true listening. Ultimately, it's about space in both the tangible, physical realm, and the intangible realm. Creating enough space to attune myself to my needs and those of my children. Space in our home, our days, our minds, our joy, our breath.*

For me this looks like creating short moments of time daily to breathe into the stomach, inhaling and exhaling with a 1-minute yoga flow while the jug boils for coffee. I honour my body and mind and consciously fill myself with empowering mantras and allow tension and limiting beliefs or anger to flow out. Allowing space in our schedule for more connection and slowness. A time for Esme and Roman to connect with their inner voices and imaginations. And space in our home - a simple, beautiful home pared back to the essential elements filled with fresh, clean air, beautifully presented toys, space on the windowsill for handmade ceramics and space on the freshly made bed for hand sewn dolls to tuck in. Space in our kitchen to enjoy simple moments - quietly chopping vegetables together, the afternoon sunlight filtering across pots of bubbling pasta. Self-care is dancing in the kitchen, being silly together, releasing tension, smiling, finding joy - allowing intuition to guide me towards stillness or movement. Ultimately living in a way that ensures I exist in the world in a way that feels natural and authentic to me.

So much of our day feels rushed: school drop off and pick up, appointments, playdates, supermarket, walking our dog, scootering - modern life is so busy that I've made it a priority to pare back as much as possible, inviting ease and beauty and turning down things that don't align. So I consciously choose and really work hard at it, how can I make this time calm, fun, positive and not filled with rushed energy? So in heavy traffic I choose not to futilely label how annoying it is and instead take several deep breaths looking up at the clouds or sing a song with Esme and Roman. It's having enough awareness of myself that I know I need to eat regularly to be less irritable. It's living with greater awareness and intention and nourishment so that I can meet the world in the lightest and most integrated way and model this to Esme and Roman. Practising moments of self-care throughout the day, every day, is a way to manage myself in a way that my highest self is proud of.

Charlotte's Top 20 Self-care Practices

So on a practical level my self-care practises are:

1. *Spending time before sleep or early in the morning to write or evoke gratitude lists*

2. *Inwardly repeating mantras and being fully present while I do daily tasks such as washing the dishes or walking down the hallway*

3. *Moving my body in a way that feels joyful, light and will brighten my energy*

4. *Dedicating 10 minutes to nourishing yoga with Indian ragas playing softly*

5. *Walking up our favourite track by the sea hand in hand with wildflowers everywhere, intentionally breathing in the fresh sea air*

6. *Savouring a glass of red wine, the early evening sun enveloping my cheeks, while Esme and Roman play around me*

7. *Dancing like no one is looking when I feel anxiety creep up so there is space for it to leave my body and mind*

8. *Eating in a balanced, healthy way with food that suits my body type and drinking plenty of water and herbal tea*

9. *Mindful consumption - of the materials we use, the toys we have, the food we nourish ourselves with, the words we converse with, the books that fill our shelves and creating an intentional window of time each day to use social media*

10. *Applying aspects of personal, spiritual development to learn as much as I can about myself and know what I can let go of that doesn't serve me (human design, To Be Magnetic neural manifestation and astrology have been instrumental for me)*

11. *Having afternoon baths with Esme and Roman with essential oils and candles and incorporating natural coffee exfoliation and oil moisturising rituals with them so that my self-care is intentionally visible*

12. *Moisturising my face and body daily with a simple mantra and massage*

13. *Watering the garden with intention or mantra*

14. *Allowing for moments of stillness by sitting alongside Esme and Roman while they play in an upright way (mostly in lotus for me), simply noticing*

15. *Mindful driving with free feelings rather than a running to do list or ruminating on old loops or conversations*

16. *Saying an inward gratitude mantra before eating my dinner*

17. *Seeing life and beauty and wonder in as many moments of the day*

18. *Reading books that support my values and nourish my mind*

19. *Cultivating a tidy, nontoxic home*

20. *Spending money on myself in a way that is truly nourishing*

I'm doing all of these things so that we can notice life in the moment we live it, approach difficulties with grace and so that I model this way of living to Esme and Roman. When I am nourished and filled up, in return, so too are they.

If you'd like to learn more from Charlotte, check her out at **@olive.and.pop** on Instagram or visit her website at **oliveandpop.com.**

@olive.and.pop

CREATE YOUR F*CKET AND FUNDAY LISTS

Grant yourself permission to care for yourself

When you're feeling guilty about scheduling in your self-care time, create your f*cket list. It could look something like this:

Example f*cket list:

- Washing clothes
- Folding clothes
- Packing away clothes
- Laundry in general
- Chores in general
- Heading somewhere just because you feel 'you have to'
- Feeling guilty for anything
- Struggling through things alone
- Justifying yourself
- Questioning yourself

And then find joy in creating your funday list!

Example funday list:

- Having brunch with friends
- Shopping
- Having alone time
- Reading at a café
- Visiting somewhere you've always wanted to, but never made the time for before
- Starting a passion project
- Creating something e.g. starting the baby book or memory box you've wanted to get to
- Growing a vege patch
- Volunteering for a cause close to your heart
- Spending time with loved ones, away from bubs

Remember mumma, filling your cup isn't selfish. It's preserving a piece of your identity and replenishing your own well-being.

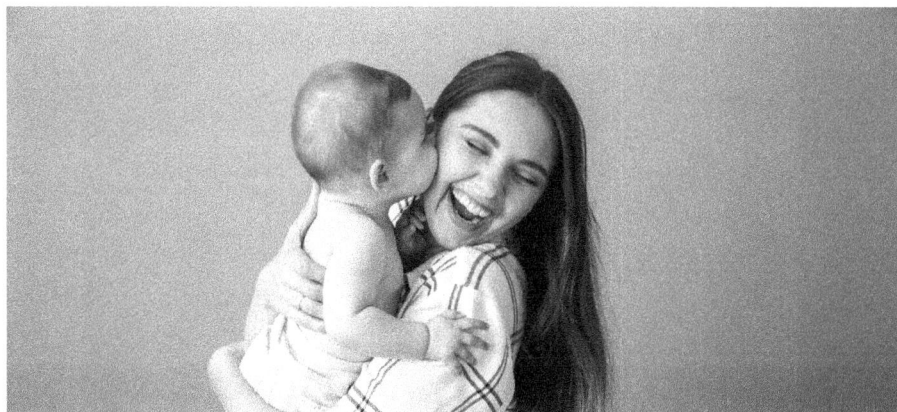

THE GRASS
IS GREENER
WHERE YOU
WATER IT

CHAPTER SIX

Nourishing your baby, your way

YOUR MENTAL HEALTH MATTERS

Firstly, I should start by saying it's important to honour your personal desires in this new world as well. If you want to learn how to breastfeed, go for it! This chapter will be most pertinent to you; but if breastfeeding is not at the top of your list, then it's okay, don't beat yourself up about it, there are other means to nourish your baby and they will grow up just fine! The world seemingly shuns mothers who feed their babies, whichever way they choose to – and isn't this just bizarre, since we're literally just FEEDING our babies, keeping them ALIVE! So concentrate on ignoring all the pests out there, and tune in with yourself. What is important to you? How do you feel about feeding your baby: do you prefer breastfeeding, bottle-feeding, or a mix of both? And then go for it, and **enjoy witnessing your baby grow up in front of you due to the incredible work YOU'RE doing!**

BREASTFEEDING AND MANAGING YOUR EXPECTATIONS

Your hormones prolactin and oxytocin are jointly responsible for this superpower – your ability to produce milk and feed your baby.

It can take a few days, even up to two weeks in some cases, for your milk to fully come in as the postpartum hormones kickstart milk production. Your baby's stomach expands from roughly the size of a toy marble at birth (which can accommodate approximately 5-7ml of milk) to the size of a ping pong ball by day 10 (which can accommodate approximately 22-27ml of milk by this stage)! This means your baby will be hungry in a short period of time - beware cluster feeding - a period when your baby wants to feed more regularly, sometimes even constantly!

The best ways to support your feeding journey:

Go with the flow and do your best to follow your baby's cues. Have a support plan and a list of numbers ready for the professionals you may need to call on - for example, lactation consultants, sleep consultants, postnatal distress counsellors, midwives or your lead maternity carer, and doulas.

Don't beat yourself up if things don't start off smoothly. Breastfeeding is a learned skill and it takes time for this new skill to feel comfortable, as it does with learning to feed out and about, navigating being semi-dressed in public, and remaining calm in times of having to provide feeds at seemingly inconvenient times - for example, having to pull over on the side of the road to calm a distressed newborn.

When nursing, get as snug as you can. Some items that can assist with your comfort include a really, supportive breastfeeding pillow and comfortable chair (one that reclines if possible) and a snack and drink station to stay nourished and hydrated. **See "Creating a Feeding Station" on page 144 at the end of this chapter.**

If you have a partner, prep them to assist with washing bottle sanitisers, pump parts and bottles as and if required.

Handover as much as you can to your partner, family or friends to support your feeding journey.

Prepare to rest. A little rest and relaxation, even if for just an hour, has been said to help milk production. Resting is truly the most important thing you can do. Leave behind the expectations to "bounce back" and give yourself permission to enjoy bonding with your baby and the time to rest.

There's support out there! Midwives or your lead maternity carer, lactation consultants and breastfeeding support groups exist to answer your questions, reassure you and offer support with feeding your baby, your way. **See "Resources" on page 227 at the end of the book.**

It's important to know that fed is best and to decide what feels right for you and your family. Breastfeeding can be a very controversial topic and it can be really hard on parents who want to breastfeed and might just really struggle to, or for those who choose and prefer not to. Either way, provided your baby is getting the sustenance it needs, that you and your lead maternity carer (LMC) are comfortable with how your baby is developing, and that you are happy with your feeding approach, then this is enough. Don't beat yourself up for not 'living up to society's expectations' (or your own previous expectations for that matter, it's alright for things to change) - this is your baby, and your feeding journey.

Wendy's wise words

Here are some famous words shared from one new mother to another, "That moment when you're discharged from the hospital and the nurse goes "you've got this!". Except you just gave birth, you haven't slept in 3 days, your vagina and nipples are destroyed and you're leaving in a diaper, with a newborn...."

- Wendy Wei Xin Poon, Founder of the Lactation Blends business, Mammas Milk Bar.

@mammasmilkbar

This very familiar scenario highlights exactly why a mother needs to be held in her postpartum period. Although medical professionals may define postpartum as the period where your body returns to its pre-pregnancy state after birth, personally, I have always felt that **postpartum ends when a mother starts feeling like herself again.** *The time when she's regaining herself and her identity after what was lost during the process of motherhood and mothering a new infant through the early years.*

There's no limit on postpartum healing. For many new mothers, postpartum is not only a time of physical changes from healing after childbirth to hormonal mood swings, but the challenges of added stress of tackling breastfeeding, sleep deprivation, and the overall monumental adjustment to motherhood.

As you can imagine, all these factors closely knit into maternal mental health at a time when a new mother can feel intense vulnerability. She herself needs to be held, nourished, and supported through this time until she feels she has adjusted to the new family dynamic.

Often when a child is born, so is a mother; postpartum is a time when she gradually becomes a mother.

Why Wendy started Mammas Milk Bar and her own challenges as a mother.

During and after my pregnancy, I struggled with boosting my breastmilk supply in a way that was natural and healthy and not relying on sweet lactation treats. I also found it hard to find clean protein powder to support my nutritional needs during pregnancy and breastfeeding that didn't have nasties and the crazy ingredients that come with commercial protein powders.

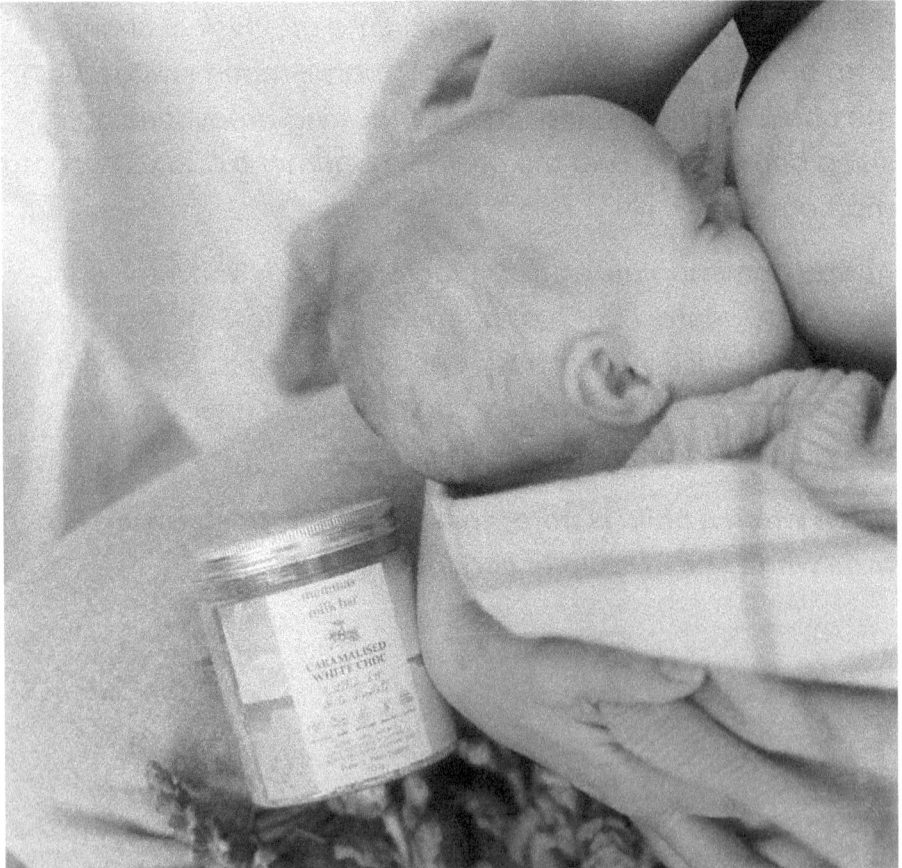

I wanted to do my best to breastfeed my baby. Needing nourishment during postpartum, I struggled to find something that was both healthy and nourishing while boosting my supply at the same time. Having to rely on lactation cookies and sugary sweets was not quite how I envisioned my postpartum diet to be, just to be able to feed my baby. As an advocate for breast is best, and with passed down knowledge of the Malaysian-Chinese traditional approach to postpartum care and nourishment, I made my own versatile blends to help solve my own problems, and I was able to exclusively breastfeed my wee babes.

Fast forward a few years to a world going through a pandemic and re-evaluating what I wanted to achieve in life, I decided to start Mammas Milk Bar with a mission to empower the motherhood journey and support every mum and newborn in being able to breastfeed and help babies be fed with the best liquid gold to ensure the best start in life.

Manage visitors' expectations.

*Although they are well-meaning, some visitors will come to see your baby but leave you feeling exhausted as you feel you need to host them. Be clear on your expectations and boundaries. **You don't have to be the hostess with the mostess!***

Make space for those visitors who gladly wash dishes, make you a meal, give you time to share your feelings and hold your baby while you take a shower, and happily give the baby back to you afterwards.

Eat healing foods.

Taking care of a wee baby and feeding requires you to eat nutritional foods and take care of yourself. Stock up your fridge, freezer and pantry with freezer meals and shelf stable foods and make sure you have supplies of maxi pads, loose fitting clothing, breast pads, and other items that help make your life a little easier in the first month or so.

Connect with professional support.

*When you're first home with a newborn, especially if you're experiencing pain or feeding is getting off to a rocky start— you'll want the right support at your fingertips. **Make a list of all your providers**—your midwife, lactation consultants, postpartum carers, perhaps a counsellor/maternal mental health provider in case the postpartum blues means you need to take extra care of your mental health.*

Time for me-time and couple time.

Try and make time everyday just for you and everyday for you and your partner. This can be tough, especially with your first baby! Your whole world has truly changed overnight.

Have a routine and make arrangements so you can enjoy a hot shower, a solo nap, a podcast, a chat with a friend, a short walk, or a hot drink.

Give yourself love.

Be kind to yourself and let others take care of you during this fleeting time. *Freely talk to everyone about how you're really feeling. Be gentle on your own expectations of yourself and baby. You don't need to be able to do everything you may set out to do,* **your best is enough.**

Being the modern mamma is really hard.

Society expects us to work as if we haven't got kids, and raise kids as if we don't need to work.

On top of that, you're expected to have a spotless house, clean laundry, to raise your kids "right", cook nutritious meals for the family, look like you have "bounced" back from pregnancy, be fit and healthy, keep good relationships going and generally have it all together.

Not to mention the expectation that all women can provide breastmilk to their babies because of our biology and the way we're made. We're expected to perform and function as per a standard textbook expectation.

The struggle to reach these expectations causes higher levels of stress, and cortisol running through the body. Not to mention unwillingly being part of the culture of a "perfect parent image norm."

SOCIETY EXPECTS US TO WORK AS IF WE HAVEN'T GOT KIDS, AND RAISE KIDS AS IF WE DON'T NEED TO WORK.

Then you have the added weight of feeling lonely, lack of sleep, feeding issues, having a crying or fussy baby, low self-esteem on baby weight and poor body image, distance from the partner/husband/family, lack of support, and worrying about caring for a new baby. Experiencing any of these pressures can impact a mother psychologically and can eventually lead to burnout.

The postpartum period is a crucial time.

This is the time when a mother learns to be a mother. Ideally she is supported by other mothers or women to develop and learn life skills and new parent education.

It's a time to recoup after carrying a baby for nine months and undergoing huge physical and hormonal changes.

It's also an opportunity for baby and mum to bond, to learn about and support breastfeeding, to establish new routines **and for mum and baby to learn about each other.**

I come from Malaysia. The biggest difference I've noticed between Eastern and Western cultures in caring for mums in the postpartum period is that in East Asian culture, the first 40 days are deeply rooted in tradition. Recipes have passed down from generation to generation to nourish new mothers.

Slowly over time, the western world has picked this up and backed tradition with science.

Western culture appears to concentrate on preparing a mother for birth, keeping a mother informed of all stages *during her pregnancy and ensuring she is well prepared for the moment baby arrives.*

Whereas in the east, there's a lot more care and focus on postpartum health *with the belief that you need to heal the body to be healthy and raise your child, as well as for strengthening your fertility for the next time you're pregnant and go through the same experience.*

In Western culture, it's relatively ok to consume ice/cold drinks during pregnancy and postpartum. But in Eastern culture, cool foods are believed to cool the womb, so warm drinks are highly encouraged throughout pregnancy and postpartum. This is because warm water simulates the same temperature as your body's core temperature, causing less physiological reaction from the body when you consume a warm drink and it works its way down the oesophagus to the stomach. A cold drink is believed to cause some physiological reaction to the body on consumption, much like somebody starting to shiver and get goosebumps if someone poured ice-cold water down their back compared with the reaction a person would get if warm water was poured over them instead.

What happens when mums have a smoother transition into motherhood...

Imagine a mother feeling nourished. A mother surrounded by a support network. A mother who feels healthier because she could go for a walk and more together after having a hot shower alone. A mother whose feeding journey is smooth because she can produce enough good quality milk to feed her baby, resulting in a better rested baby.

> **When the pain points of postpartum are addressed, I've seen mothers recover from postnatal depression and post-traumatic stress disorder and face life with so much love and positivity.**

The effect of a happier mum ripples out to create a better relationship with their husband or partner, a stronger bond between mum and baby, less anxious kids, and it can even help lessen generational trauma. ***That's the power of supporting and holding mums in the postpartum period.***

CREATING A FEEDING STATION

Here is a list of items that you can put together to create a Nursing Station:

Comfortable chair	Choose a chair with adequate back support and armrests. A rocking or gliding chair can also be helpful.
Nursing pillow	A nursing pillow can help support your baby during breastfeeding and help prevent back pain.
Footstool	A footstool can help you maintain good posture while breastfeeding and prevent back pain.
Table	Keep a table nearby to hold any items you may need, such as a glass of water, snacks, or a burp cloth.
Breast pads	Keep breast pads on hand to prevent leaks and keep your clothing dry. Reuseable breast pads are great!
Lanolin cream	Lanolin cream can help soothe sore or cracked nipples.
Nursing bra or top	Wear a comfortable nursing bra or top that allows easy access for breastfeeding.
Water bottle	Stay hydrated by keeping a water bottle nearby or many.

Snacks	Keep healthy snacks on hand to help maintain your energy levels. Nuts are a great source of omega-3 which supports oestrogen levels.
Burp cloths	Keep a few burp cloths nearby to clean up any spit-up or spills.
Breast pump	If you plan to pump breast milk, keep a breast pump nearby along with any necessary accessories.
Nipple shields	Nipple shields can help with sore or cracked nipples or if your baby is having difficulty latching. You may want to discuss this with a lactation consultant before starting use of them.
Breast milk storage bags or containers	If you plan to pump breast milk, keep breast milk storage bags or containers nearby for safe and convenient storage.

Remember that this list is not exhaustive, and every mum and baby are different. You may find that you need additional items or prefer to keep some items in a different location.

"AH BABIES! THEY'RE MORE THAN JUST ADORABLE LITTLE CREATURES ON WHOM YOU CAN BLAME YOUR FARTS!"

– Tina Fey, Actress and Comedian

CHAPTER SEVEN

Postpartum Nutrition

NOURISHMENT OVER PERFECTION

Postpartum Nutrition made easy!

"Nourishing your body with nutrient-dense foods is one of the most important considerations for your postpartum recovery. You've just grown a human; you're physically recovering from labour, and lactation is placing increased demands on your body. Food should not add to the stress – focus on 'nourishing' you and your baby, not striving for 'perfect' nutrition."

– Amanda Bennett, Public Nutritionist and Founder of The Natal Nutritionist.
@thenatalnutritionist

Here's the thing mumma, after you give birth to your beautiful bub, your body is in recovery mode. At the same time, sleep deprivation and the general demands that come with raising a baby can make you feel like you're running a marathon. No wonder you feel so hungry and thirsty all the time, and if you're breastfeeding, this can affect you even more.

> Although it can be tricky to deal with all the challenges a newborn brings with it, focusing on eating the right foods and drinking enough water should be a key priority for your postpartum recovery, particularly during the Fourth Trimester. Your body needs fuel and energy. Unless you're allergic to anything, don't deprive yourself of certain food groups because you and your baby might miss out on vital nutrients.

Staying nourished and hydrated makes everything that little bit easier - it gives you more energy, helps to regulate your hormones, and in turn can help with your mood, sleep, your milk production, and overall recovery.

If you're worried about your baby developing allergies, removing allergen foods from your diet like nuts, dairy and gluten **doesn't reduce the risk.**

Try and have a flexible meal plan so you know that you're getting the right foods. When you're tired and want a quick hit, it's so tempting to reach for sugary or fatty food. It's normal, but a little forward planning can mean you're getting the right, nutrient-dense foods that keep you going longer

- nourishing you so that you can nourish your baby. But mumma, remember perfect is impossible. You're not always going to have balanced meals. Try to select a variety of foods that are rich in vitamins and minerals and high in fibre as much as you can.

AMANDA'S TOP POSTPARTUM NUTRITION TIPS

Set up a meal roster with willing friends and family members. *This can spread the load and make your friends, neighbours, colleagues, and family feel like they are doing something that's really, helpful and practical.*

Slow-cooked meals are winners. *Chuck everything in before lunchtime – or ask your visitors or partner to assist with the prepping - and you'll have a delicious and nutritious meal waiting for you when you're ready.*

Breastfeeding/pumping and your recovery is thirsty work. *Keep a water bottle beside you at all times, one that you can easily use one-handed. I know that caffeine is tempting but try to limit this because it dehydrates you and can make you feel stressed and anxious. One way to know if you're dehydrated is to check the colour of your urine. Pale yellow? You're good. Any darker and you need to drink more water.*

Choose foods from the four groups below that you enjoy. *The key is that they're simple – you don't want to spend hours in the kitchen. Tell your friends and family about the foods you like, so that each time you have a visitor they can bring you a meal or key items to help stock your fridge or pantry.*

Concentrate on eating a variety of foods:

Grain foods including complex carbs

Think pasta, rice, bread, cereals, quinoa, oats, and polenta. Here you get your lovely complex carbs, protein, fibre, vitamins, and minerals including vitamin B, folate, magnesium and zinc. Choose grainy breads over white bread because they keep you fuller for longer.

Fruit and veggies

Veggies and fruit are jam-packed with vitamins and minerals to help protect and nourish our bodies in various ways. "Eat the rainbow" to boost your immunity and give you a happy digestive system. Where you can, go for whole fruit rather than juiced or dried fruit.

Protein

Protein helps repair tissue, produce collagen, and balance our hormones. Choose lean meat and poultry, as well as a variety of oily fish, eggs, tofu, nuts, seeds and legumes or beans. Protein also provides iodine, zinc, vitamin B12 and essential fatty acids.

Milky products

Milk, cheese, and yoghurt provide calcium in a way that's easy and quick for your body to absorb. Calcium is super important for bub's bone development and is a key part of breastmilk. Dairy products also contain protein, iodine, vitamins A, D and B12 and Zinc. **If your Lead Maternity Carer (LMC) suggests removing dairy from your diet for a period to support your baby's digestive system for example, you can still absorb the nutrients you require through other milky products** such as coconut, soy or oat milk, and coconut yogurt to name a few. Discuss how to get sufficient calcium intake with your LMC, and medical professional or nutritionist, if you have any concerns and are removing dairy from your diet, or you yourself may be dairy intolerant.

"Mums are telling me one of the big things is food. We are very hungry postpartum. While we are holding our babies and nurturing our babies, who's holding and nurturing us as parents?

As a postpartum doula, one of our roles is to look after the mum. And that's wrapping around the birthing family, supporting the birthing person so that they can rest, recover, and have a start into parenthood that is blissful. And that means good nutrition, nutrient-dense food, slow cooked. So that's really nourishing for the body and for the joints so that they can recover."

- Shelly Mackie, Doula in Christchurch, New Zealand.

Consider the key nutrients required, particularly if you are breastfeeding:

- **Calcium**
- **Iodine**
- **Vitamin B12**
- **Vitamin D**
- **Iron**
- **Healthy Fats (e.g olive, coconut and avacado oil)**
- **Water**

Amanda states,

> **The good news is if you are eating a balanced diet with a variety of foods from each of the food groups, you will likely be getting enough of most nutrients. However, there are a few key nutrients you need to be aware of if you are breastfeeding (as above).**

AMANDA'S TOP SNACK SUGGESTIONS FOR POSTPARTUM MUMS

- Wholegrain bread with natural nut butter (peanut, almond, etc.)
- Carrot, celery and/or capsicum sticks and hummus
- Smoothie **(check out Amanda's Hulk Smoothie recipe)**
- Banana bread **(check out Amanda's Banana & Coconut Bread recipe)**
- Greek yoghurt with muesli/granola and fresh fruit
- Wholegrain crackers with cheese and tomato
- Boiled eggs
- Piece of fruit with nut butter or yoghurt
- Trail mix **(check out Pip's Mumma's Muesli)**
- Edamame beans
- Avocado on rice cakes
- Popcorn

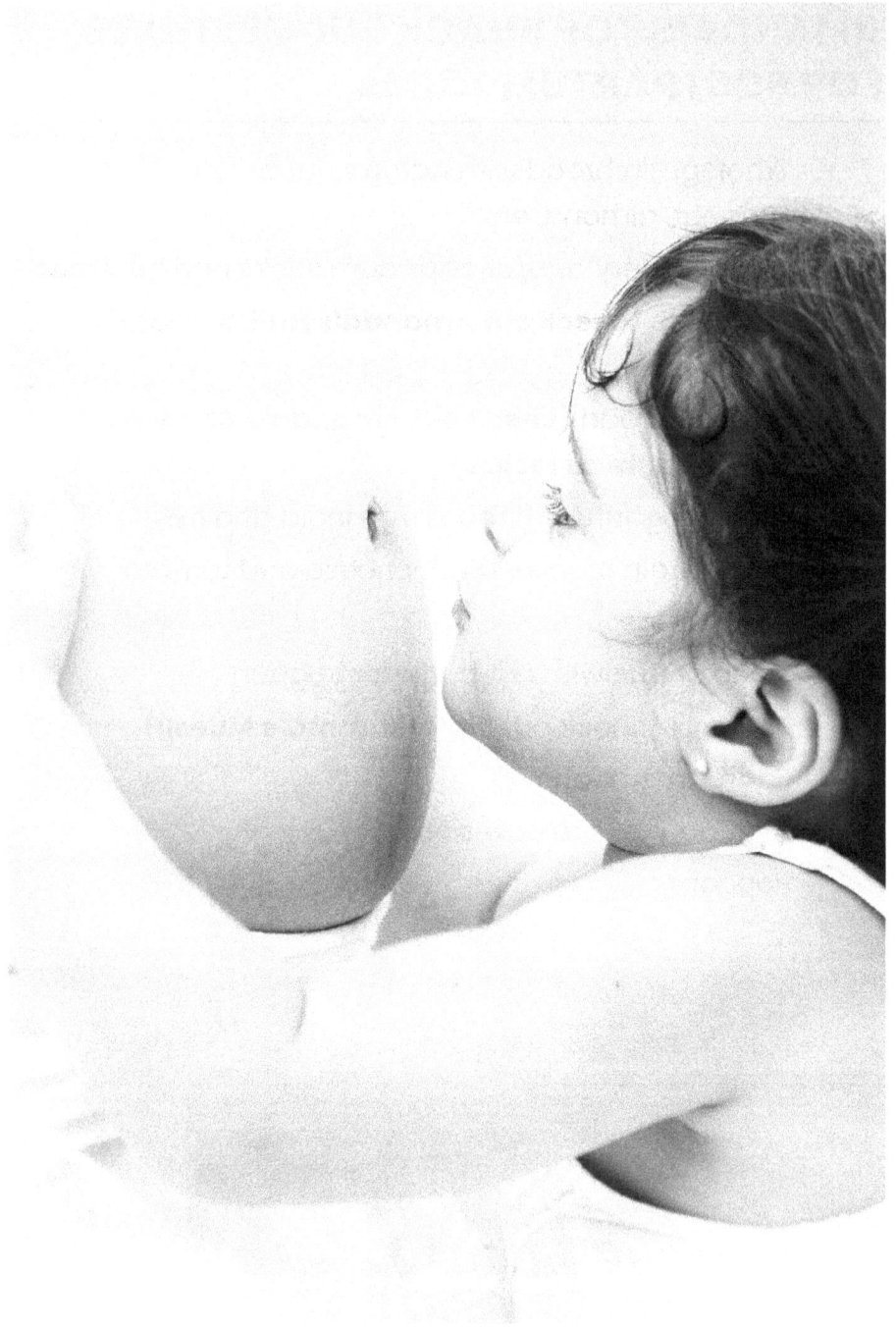

Recipes to Rebuild postpartum Mums

AMANDA'S HULK SMOOTHIE

Ingredients	Method
1. 200ml milk or milk alternative	Put all ingredients except chia seeds into a blender and blend!
2. 1 frozen banana	
3. 1 TBSP peanut butter	Pour into glass then sprinkle the chia seeds on top and mix through.
4. 1 handful of washed baby spinach leaves	
5. 1 tsp chia seeds	Enjoy!

AMANDA'S BANANA & COCONUT BREAD

Ingredients	Method
1. 1 1/2 cups gluten-free plain flour	Preheat oven to 180C. Grease and line the base and 2 long sides of an 11cm x 20cm loaf pan.
2. 1 cup desiccated coconut	
3. 1/3 cup brown sugar	Combine dry ingredients.
4. 2 tsp gluten-free baking powder	Combine wet ingredients. Add to dry ingredients.
5. 1/2 tsp bicarb soda	Pour into loaf pan and bake for 1 hour or until skewer inserted into the centre comes out clean.
6. 1/4 tsp salt	
7. 1 1/2 cups mashed banana	
8. 2/3 cup olive oil	Once cooked set aside for 5 mins before turning out onto cooling rack.
9. 2 eggs or equivalent egg replacer	

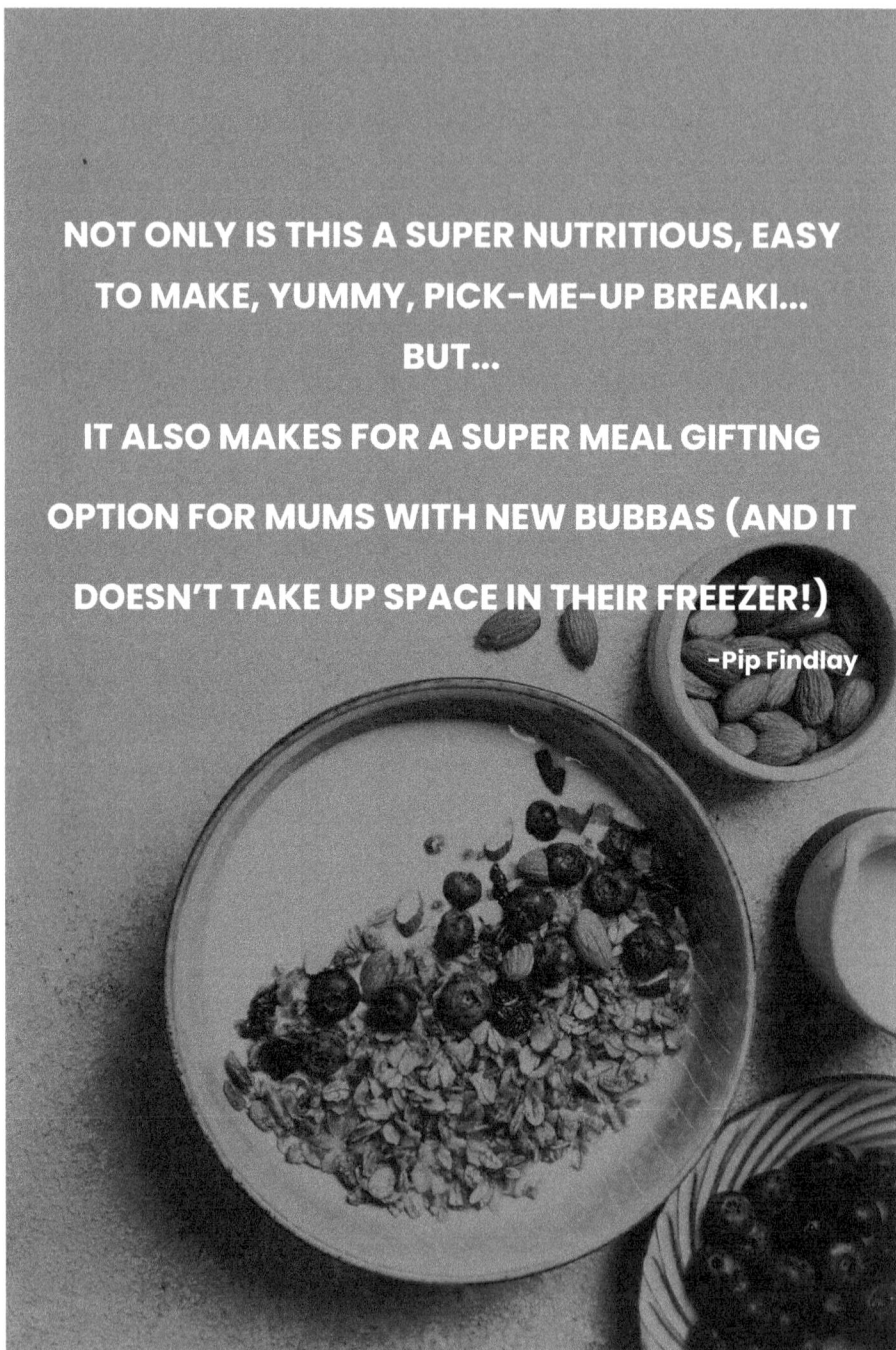

**NOT ONLY IS THIS A SUPER NUTRITIOUS, EASY TO MAKE, YUMMY, PICK-ME-UP BREAKI...
BUT...**

IT ALSO MAKES FOR A SUPER MEAL GIFTING OPTION FOR MUMS WITH NEW BUBBAS (AND IT DOESN'T TAKE UP SPACE IN THEIR FREEZER!)

-Pip Findlay

PIP'S MUMMA'S MUESLI

Ingredients

1. 4 cups of rolled oats
2. 2 cups of chia seeds
3. 1 cup ground LSA (Linseed, Sunflower seed and Almond mix)
4. 1 cup sunflower seeds
5. 1 cup pumpkin seeds
6. 1/2 cup sultanas
7. 1/2 cup dried cranberries
8. 1/2 cup banana chips
9. 1 cup dessicated coconut
10. 2-3 TBSP of syrup of choice
11. 2 tsp ground cinnamon
12. 2 cups chopped almonds

Method

Add it all together.

Throw it in the oven at 200 degree C for 20 min with turning it over part way at the ten minute mark.

Continue to keep an eye on it. It can burn quickly so just hang out in the kitchen while you are making it.

It's ready when it's golden brown on top and the oats have slightly hardened.

Add the banana chips in at the end!

Every batch I make turns out slightly different because I never pay attention to how much I'm really adding of anything, so experiment and have fun!

Recipe inspired by The Australian Women's Weekly 'Sugar Free' Cookbook published in 2015 (Recipe: Chia & Almond Toasted Muesli pg 12)

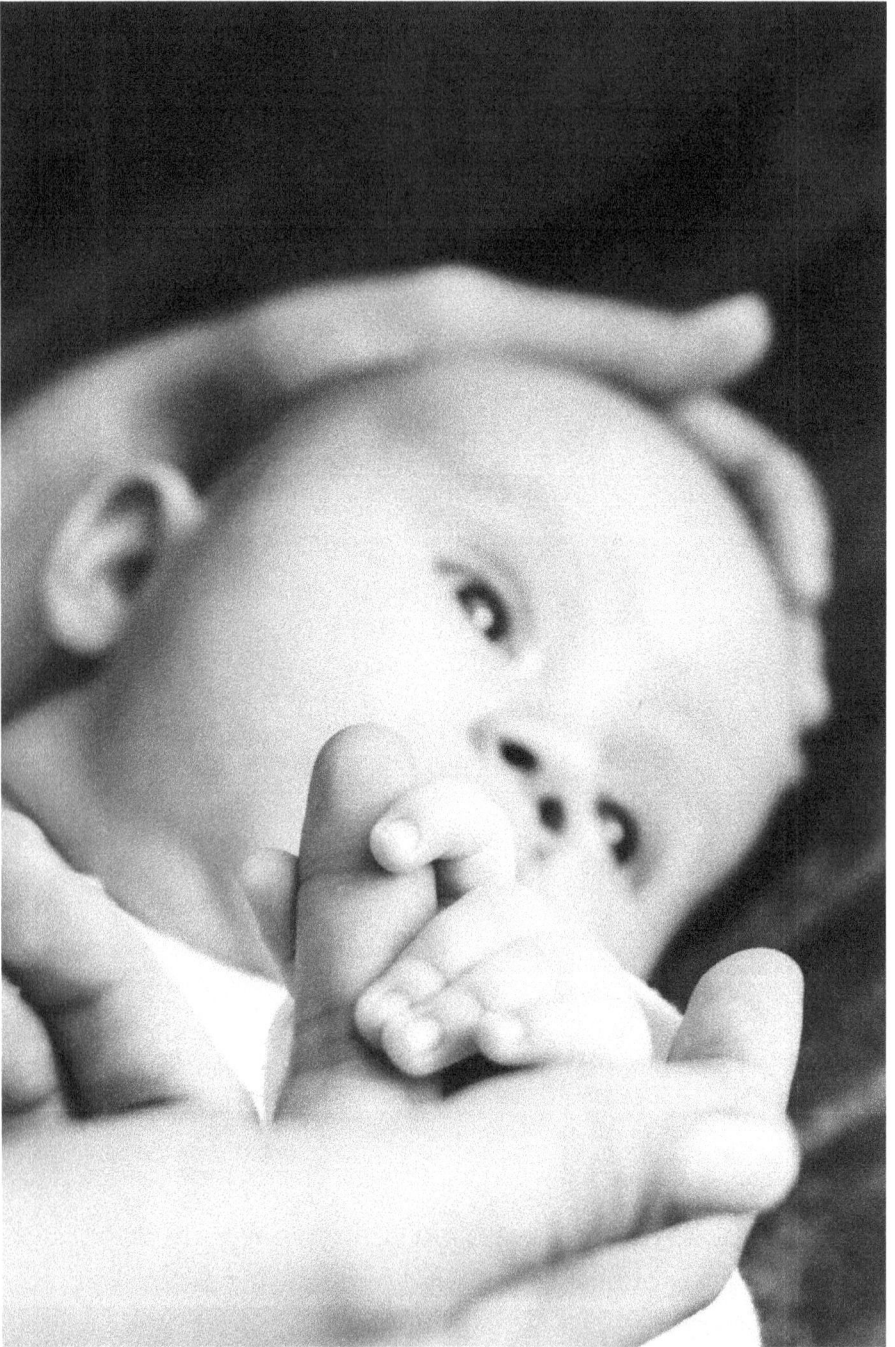

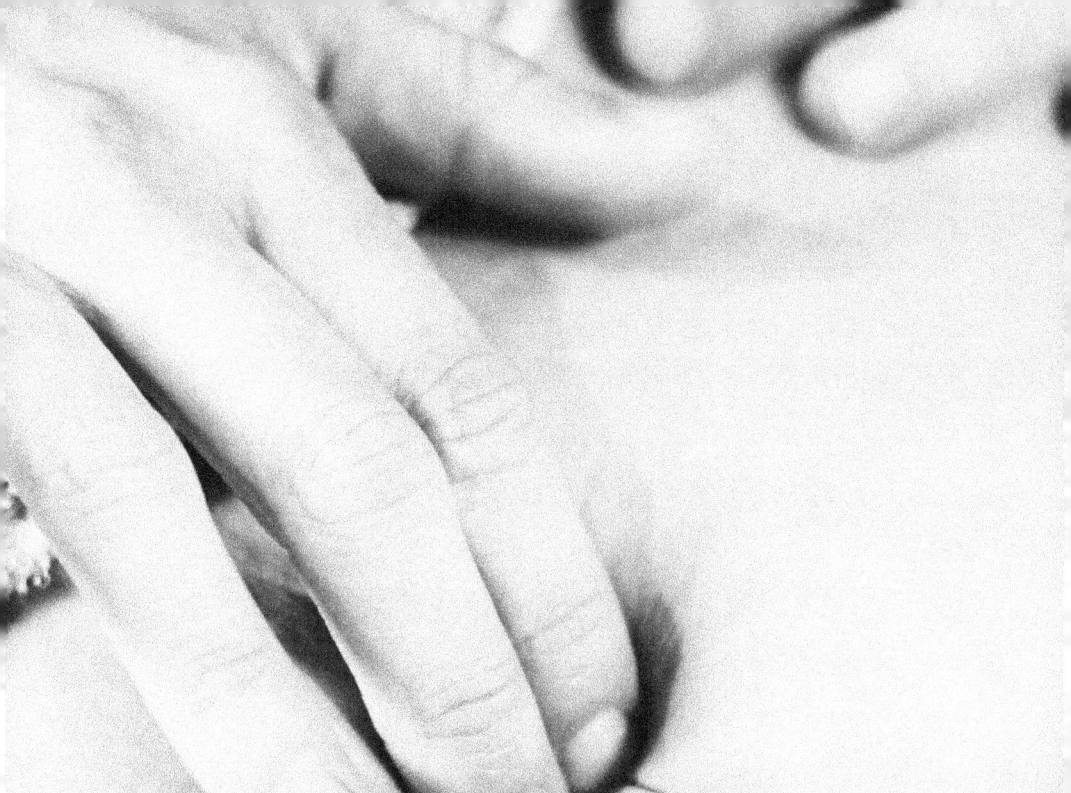

CHAPTER EIGHT

Pelvic Health and Exercise

TAKING CARE OF YOUR PELVIC HEALTH

C-section or vaginal birth
Avoid sneeze and wee's, painful sex and more

"Your pelvic floor muscles support your bladder, bowels and uterus, keeping these organs up inside of you, and stop leakage of urine and faeces. They support your lower back and pelvic joints and give you sexual function. These muscles get weaker from pregnancy and birth and need to be retrained no matter how you delivered your baby."

– From Sophie Fogarty, senior pelvic floor therapist and co-founder of Unity Studios.

Unity Studios, based in Auckland, NZ, is a space that provides exercise classes, rehab Pilates and physiotherapy to help women through their pregnancy and postnatal recovery journeys.

@unitystudiosnz

Most of us have heard the joke that trampolines and even coughing or sneezing are a no-go for mums if we don't want to pee ourselves.

But your pelvic floor does so much more than stopping you wetting yourself. A strong and flexible pelvic floor also means less pain, better back support, better sex, and overall being able to lead a fulfilling lifestyle (including being able to jump on the trampoline with your kids, without the fear of experiencing incontinence!). It's important that we look after our pelvic floor – especially after pregnancy and birth when it's been through such a lot.

Did you know that...

- One-third of women in New Zealand who have carried a baby will leak and experience incontinence.
- Half of women live with some degree of prolapse i.e., when your uterus, bowels or bladder has descended to some degree into your vaginal canal.
- A quarter of women live with bladder and or bowel incontinence.
- A fifth of women report pain during sex.

Source: Continence.org.nz, 2020

These are grossly high stats, and they shouldn't be normalised. During pregnancy, you may have experienced a few mishaps when you coughed or sneezed. But once you've had your baby, this shouldn't be allowed to be your new normal.

Although it can be almost bearable immediately after birth, if you don't build up the strength in your pelvic floor, your health condition will drastically change in future years. Many women end up seeing pelvic floor physiotherapists when their children have grown up. It's hitting them so much worse in the later years and it could have been prevented.

You may have heard of pelvic floor therapists, or women's health physio's, and the incredible work that they do in supporting women in strengthening their pelvic floor, so you can lead a happy, healthy lifestyle and be fully involved with your kids.

I personally deal with pelvic issues, which is why I'm such an advocate for pelvic floor therapists. I have incredible professionals supporting me (thank you Sophie & Caitlin from Unity Studios!) and I am spreading the awareness. I sincerely recommend that you see one.

Your pelvic floor is your body's version of a Swiss army knife and supports you in many areas. It helps with your bladder and bowel movements, through to your actual core and your ability to stand up, to move around and stay upright. **If you've got a strong pelvic floor and a strong core, your body works in harmony, including healthy bodily functions and being able to enjoy sex.**

YOUR PELVIC FLOOR MUSCLES GET
WEAKER FROM PREGNANCY AND BIRTH

- Sophie Fogarty, SNR Pelvic Floor Therapist.

DID YOU KNOW THAT YOUR PELVIC FLOOR MUSCLES NEED TO BE RE-TRAINED REGARDLESS OF WHETHER YOU GIVE BIRTH VAGINALLY OR HAVE A C-SECTION BUB?

It's not just childbirth that causes weakness of your pelvic floor. During pregnancy, hormones released like relaxin cause your pelvic floor to become more stretchy, and the increased load from the baby causes the muscles to lengthen and weaken.

You may have heard about abdominal separation, or diastasis recti. Your six pack muscles have to separate during pregnancy to allow room for your growing baby. **This is a completely normal part of pregnancy and isn't something to be feared.** In fact, 100% of women will have experienced this after giving birth. The muscles largely come together postnatally but in most cases the gap won't close completely and is likely to get larger with each pregnancy. Pelvic floor physios are able to guide women on safe abdominal strengthening to help women to gradually build up their core strength and bring the muscles together. **Each woman is different so an individualised exercise programme is ideal.**

The splitting of the abdominals is so that you can grow your belly and make room for the baby. **It should resolve itself naturally, but if it doesn't, I highly encourage you to get help,** especially as if you don't get onto it, you may start to treat it as your new normal.

I was that person with my first baby. My stomach flattened when I'd lie down but a Toblerone-shape would appear when I'd sit upright. I thought this was normal. And it most certainly wasn't. Unfortunately this resulted in a stomach hernia before I'd had the chance to seek sufficient treatment.

We shouldn't be experiencing these hardships and letting them adversely affect our lifestyle. If you're ever concerned, talk up, and if you can, seek help from a pelvic floor therapist to support you.

The good news is you can retrain your pelvic floor.

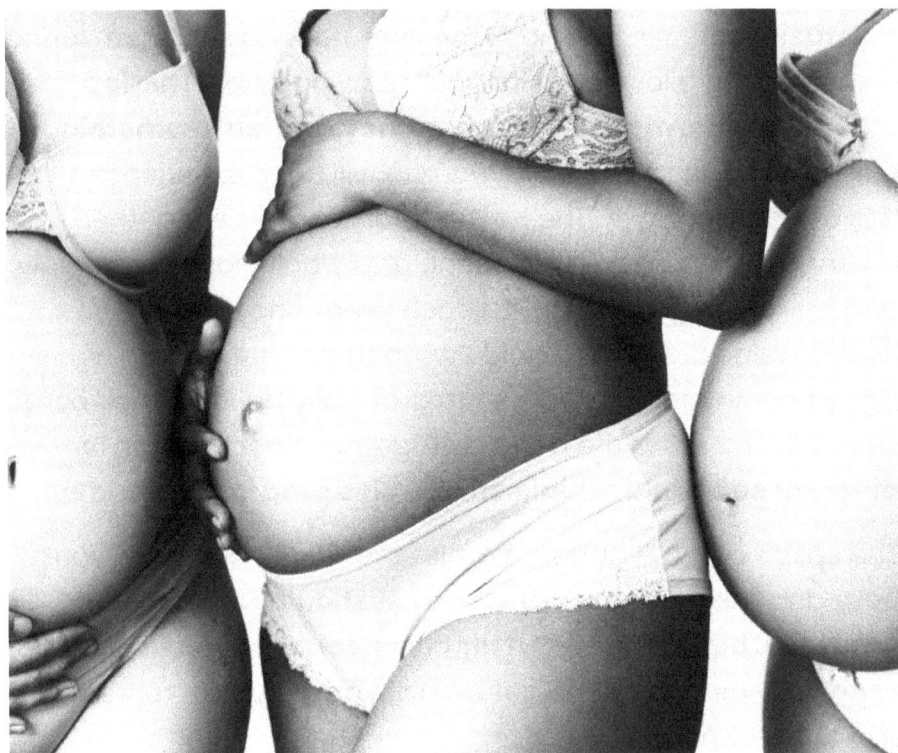

Sophie Fogarty, Senior Pelvic Floor Therapist, gives this advice after birth, in an easy to recall acronym, RICE:

R

> *Rest. Lie down, mumma. Being horizontal as much as you can for the first week post-birth is the best way to rest and heal your pelvic floor.*

I

> *Ice, ice, baby. That's right, place some ice on your perineum every two hours if you can to reduce pain, swelling and bruising. You can also put your pads in the freezer (see "How to make a DIY padsicle for your vajazzicle" on page 178 and a handy "Birth Recovery Checklist" on page 180 at the end of this chapter).*

C

> *Compression. Don't wear knickers that are oversized or have lost their elastic. Put on some firm, supportive undies. You can also wear an abdominal tubigrip or postnatal recovery garment to help your abs heal too.*

E

> *Exercise. No don't rush off to bootcamp. We're talking kegels. It's safe and recommended to start your pelvic floor kegels the day after you deliver. Read on to learn about safely returning to exercise in your postpartum.*

When should you see a pelvic floor therapist?

You can consult a pelvic floor therapist while you're pregnant, as once you return after birth, they'll be able to identify the change that your body has gone through and how to best support you in your post recovery.

> Pelvic health physio has been proven to reduce the risk of perineal tears during birth, and also help with bladder and bowel leakage, vaginal prolapse symptoms, painful sex and the aches and pains of pregnancy and parenting.

The pelvic floor needs to be strong and flexible for birth to allow the baby to move down the birth canal. Pelvic floor physios can identify those who have a tense and tight pelvic floor and support them throughout their pregnancy with pelvic floor relaxation breathing, perineal massage and stretches. Learning to relax the pelvic floor well can reduce the risk of having a larger tear and an instrumental delivery.

YOUR POSTNATAL WARRANT OF FITNESS (WOF)

After birth, the guideline recommendation is that you see a pelvic floor physio at the six-week mark for your postnatal WOF (Warrant Of Fitness). I've spoken with many practitioners, who recommend that you visit as soon as you're ready, which could even be as early as four weeks.

A vaginal birth can commonly result in a birth injury. Pelvic floor dysfunction such as bladder or bowel leakage, constipation, vaginal prolapse causing heaviness or dragging, and painful sex are common but are definitely not normal. It's also important to see a pelvic floor physio if you have any of these symptoms or if you have had an instrumental delivery (forceps or ventouse), a larger tear (3 and 4 degree), you were pushing for more than 2 hours or had a baby weighing over 4kg. Pelvic physios can also help with common complaints like back, neck and pelvic joint pain (often arising from poor breastfeeding postures) and recti diastasis.

What to expect from a pelvic floor therapist

Your pelvic floor physio, also referred to as a women's health physio, will assess your pelvic floor via real-time ultrasound or perform a vaginal examination, do an assessment of your abdominal muscles, your posture and your general strength. **A vaginal examination of the pelvic floor gives more information than an ultrasound** and your physio will be able to look at any scar tissue, assess for prolapse and look at the strength, tone and flexibility of your pelvic floor.

You'll be provided with an individualised exercise programme to help you to achieve your goals and to safely return to the exercise or hobbies you love.

SAFELY RETURNING TO EXERCISE IN YOUR POSTPARTUM

When to exercise again after birth and what to do is a common question from new parents.

WEEK 1

In the first week following birth, pure rest is recommended. It's suggested that you continue your kegels from 48 hours following birth, but if you're not up for this, don't stress. Rest is best! Recall Sophie's acronym RICE!

WEEKS 1 - 6

Between the first- and six-weeks following birth, gentle walks are recommended. Of course, this depends entirely on how you're feeling, and what kind of birth you're recovering from. Pelvic floor exercises, namely kegels, are advised to be done 3 times/day so doing them when feeding will mean you're killing two birds with one stone!

WEEKS 6 – 12

From six weeks onwards, low impact exercise such as Pilates and yoga are advised, but it's still too early to hit fast-paced aerobics classes!

For the duration of your Fourth Trimester, the first 12 weeks following birth, it's suggested that all forms of running and high impact exercise like HIIT be kept at bay. Running tends to add heightened pressure on your pelvic floor, so you're at risk of further weakening your pelvic floor if you engage in this activity as your pelvic floor is still fragile and in recovery mode.

And remeber, it can take up to five months after having your baby for your relaxin levels to stabalize, so at this point you are still prone to spraining or overstretching your muscles and jeopardizing your joint health.

POST 12 WEEKS

If you want to get back into running later down the track, there are special guides to help you slowly progress back into running, with instructions on how to protect your pelvic floor as best as possible. Again, seeking the help of a pelvic floor therapist to do a return to running assessment will support you in a personalised treatment and exercise plan to get you back into running in no time.

Until then, take it easy mumma! Rest up, and book in that appointment with your local pelvic floor therapist..

HOW TO MAKE A DIY PADSICLE FOR YOUR VAJAZZICLE

A spa day for your downstairs

Padsicles, essentially postpartum pads, are designed to help soothe your downstairs' and tooshi's pains that you will likely experience after the birth of your baby.

> They are referred to as padsicles because they are frozen pads, which provide the cooling relief and support in reducing swelling that your nether regions are in much need of.

Often witch hazel, aloe vera gel, and key essential oils are added onto the pads for additional recovery aid. When purchasing these items, look for unscented, alcohol-free products.

Also, this is a great job for your partner to learn! You have enough going on with trying to learn how to mother and nourish your newborn, that making padsicles should sit alongside getting the nappy-bag packed. You can even print this very page out for your partner and stick it on the fridge!

Hint hint!...

What you'll need:

- Maternity pads
- Aloe Vera Gel – antiseptic
- Perineal spray / Witch Hazel – provides a numbing effect
- Optional: Essential Oils (Tea tree oil, lavender oil)
- A freezer!

How to make your DIY padsicles:

1. Wash your hands.

2. Unwrap a few maternity pads at a time, but don't throw away the wrappers – you'll need to reattach these to the pads once you've added the gel & oils, before you place them in the freezer, so they don't stick to each other!

3. Smear roughly a tablespoon of aloe vera gel along the maternity pad from top to bottom, sticking within the centre of the pad. Be careful not to add too much as it may spill out the sides as it defrosts when you're wearing it later.

4. Add a quick spray of your perineal spray, or witch hazel spray mixture (half witch hazel, half water, with a few drops of your preferred essential oils), onto the pad.

5. Let the pads dry for a few minutes.

6. Place the wrappers back onto them.

7. Freeze the pads, and they're DONE!

Now when you're in need of a cool-down, you can rest assured you'll be ready!

BIRTH RECOVERY CHECKLIST

- ☐ High-waisted undies (especially for c-sections)
- ☐ Maternity Pads (postpartum bleeding: 2-6 weeks)
- ☐ Hydrogel breast pads or cabbage leaves (for engorged breasts)
- ☐ Lanolin cream (for cracked nipples)
- ☐ Breast pads (for milk leaks)
- ☐ Aloe vera gel or Tea tree oil (antiseptic - create your padsicles!)
- ☐ Witch hazel spray (to soothe hemorrhoids, & creams are available)
- ☐ Arnica oil or tablets (reduce internal swelling)
- ☐ Peri-bottle (a waterbottle works just fine too!)
- ☐ Clay ice pack (reduce swelling)
- ☐ Heat pack (for uterus contractions)
- ☐ Tissue oil (to reduce scarring)
- ☐ Items to assist with constipation (prune/ kiwi juice, fibre rich snacks)

OTHER

- ☐ Nipple sheilds
- ☐ Belly Band or tubigrip
- ☐ Donut cushion (possibly worth considering if you have a vaginal birth, but discuss with your LMC)
- ☐ Other suppliments: iron tablets,omega 3 fatty acids pills (and prescribed pain medication)

CHAPTER NINE

NINE

A plan to thrive

The Fourth Trimester, or postpartum period, can be a challenging time for many new mothers as they adjust to their new role and recover from childbirth. It's important to prioritize self-care during this time to help you feel good and rebuild yourself.

Read on to discover a 12-week plan with one thing to focus on each day to help you thrive in your Fourth Trimester. The most important thing is to prioritize your self-care and focus on one thing at a time to help you thrive during the postpartum period.

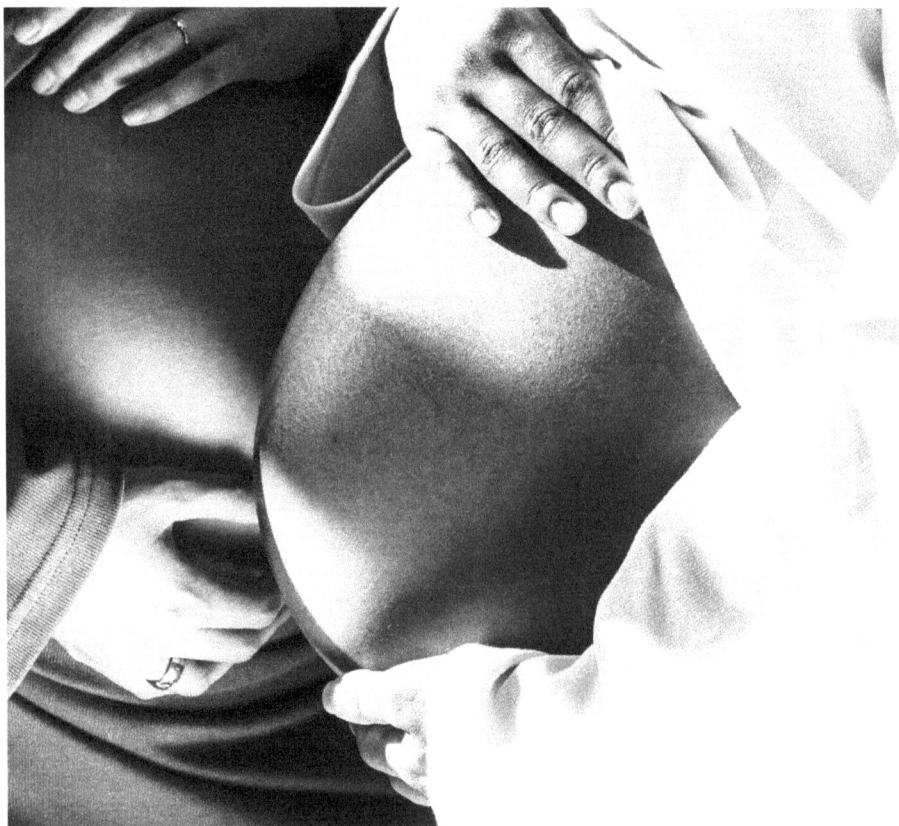

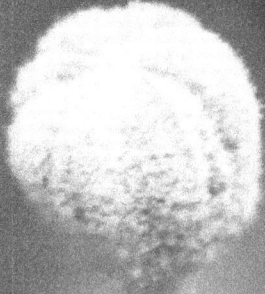

Month one

Week 1
Rest and Recovery

Day 1	Take a nap whenever you're able to!
Day 2	Drink plenty of water and eat nourishing foods.
Day 3	Accept help from family and friends.
Day 4	Write down your birth story before you forget details.
Day 5	Take a warm bath or shower with essential oils.
Day 6	Wear comfortable clothing, it's ok to have a PJ day (always).
Day 7	Organise a newborn photoshoot.

See "Chapter 8" on page 165 to become acquainted with the RICE acronym, how to make your own DIY padsicles, and the birth recovery checklist.

Week 2
Baby Bonding

Day 8	Spend quality time with your baby.
Day 9	Read a book or sing a lullaby to your baby.
Day 10	Do some skin-to-skin time with your baby.
Day 11	Get some Vit D, breathe in some fresh air, and head out on a stroll.
Day 12	Attend a new mum support group or coffee group class.
Day 13	Create a special bonding routine with your baby.
Day 14	Document your baby's latest milestones.

See "15 Ways to Bond with your baby" on page 83 at the end of chapter 3.

Week 3
Emotional Well-Being

Day 15	Reach out to a loved one, therapist or counsellor to talk with.
Day 16	Journal how your first couple weeks post-baby have been.
Day 17	Connect with other new mums or your coffee group.
Day 18	Talk openly with your partner about your feelings.
Day 19	Take a break from social media, book in that appointment with your Pelvic Floor Therapist for the 6-week mark.
Day 20	Practice gratitude.
Day 21	Do something that makes you laugh.

See"15 Ways to raise your Oxytocin Levels" on page 63 at the end of chapter 2.

Week 4
Sleep

Day 22	Develop a bedtime routine.
Day 23	Take a warm bath before bed.
Day 24	Create a sleep-friendly environment.
Day 25	Avoid using electronics before bed.
Day 26	Try a relaxation technique.
Day 27	Practice good sleep hygiene.
Day 28	Take a nap during the day.

See "9 Ways to Improve Sleep" on page 37 in chapter 1.

Month two

Week 5
Nutrition

Day 29	Create a meal plan for the week.
Day 30	Cook a healthy meal.
Day 31	Try bake Pip's Mummas' Muesli.
Day 32	Have a nutritious snack.
Day 33	Try a new recipe, what about Amanda's Hulk Smoothie?
Day 34	Stay hydrated.
Day 35	Limit caffeine intake.

See Chapter 7 "Postpartum Nutrition" on page 147.

Learn more about nutritional literacy and grab your handy, done-for-you shopping guide via the Fourth Trimester Toolkit course at WILDBEGINNINGS.THINKIFIC.COM.

Week 6
Self-Care

Day 36	Get a haircut or a new style.
Day 37	Get a pedi, massage or spa treatment.
Day 38	Take a relaxing bath with essential oils.
Day 39	Do something you love.
Day 40	Get dressed up and go out for a date day with your partner.
Day 41	Buy yourself something that will make you feel good about yourself.
Day 42	Take a day off just for yourself.

See Chapter 5 "Self-care" on page 113.

Further deepdive with a certified life coach into how you can effectively practice self care, and grab your self-care tracker, via our Fourth Trimester Toolkit at WILDBEGINNINGS.THINKIFIC. COM. Start to fill your cup today!

Week 7
Physical Exercise

Day 43	Try a gentle yoga class (post 6 weeks, low impact exercise is safe).
Day 44	Go for a walk with your baby.
Day 45	Sign up for a low impact postpartum exercise class.
Day 46	Do some stretching exercises.
Day 47	Practice Kegel exercises.
Day 48	Dance to your favourite music.
Day 49	Take a rest day.

See Chapter 8 "Pelvic Health and Exercise" on page 165.

For more safe-at home postpartum and relaxing visualisation exercise videos from the experts (a pelvic floor therapist, postnatal certified personal trainer and a somatics educator & instructor), check out our Fourth Trimester Toolkit course at WILDBEGINNINGS.THINKIFIC.COM.

Week 8
Relationships

Day 50	Eat dinner at the table with your partner, no TV or phones!
Day 51	Connect with a friend.
Day 52	Call a family member.
Day 53	Write a letter to baby for them to read when they're older.
Day 54	Go on a family outing.
Day 55	Have a picnic in the park.
Day 56	Send someone a care package.

Deepdive into your relationships & learn more from a professional life coach about setting boundries, tools to help you cope with navigating changing relationships, asking for and accepting help, understanding the five love languages and your 'new' relationship with your partner. Check out our Fourth Trimester Toolkit course at WILDBEGINNINGS.THINKIFIC. COM.

Month three

Week 9
Mindfulness

Day 57	Practice mindful breathing.
Day 58	Do a guided meditation.
Day 59	Talk to a trusted friend or family member about your feelings.
Day 60	Read a book or watch a movie that inspires you.
Day 61	Write in a journal and reflect on your emotions up to this point.
Day 62	Take a break from social media and screen time.
Day 63	Compliment yourself on five things you're proud about, being YOU.

To gain access to a handy visualisation audio recording to help you to practice full relaxation through a 7 minute hip-shoulder release, designed by a somatics educator & instructor, visit our online course The Fourth Trimester Toolkit at WILDBEGINNINGS.THINKIFIC.COM.

Week 10
Hobbies and Interests

Day 64	Pick up a hobby you used to enjoy.
Day 65	Try a new hobby or activity.
Day 66	Attend a class or workshop.
Day 67	Find a new café to visit.
Day 68	Listen to a podcast or audiobook.
Day 69	Go somewhere you have never been before.
Day 70	Try a new nature trail for your planned walk with bubs.

Deepdive into your identity with a certified life coach to better help you to embrace the "new you", with a handy downloadable PDF to guide you through better understanding your core values via our online Fourth Trimester Toolkit course at WILDBEGINNINGS.THINKIFIC.COM.

Week 11
Productivity

Day 71	Set achievable goals for the week.
Day 72	Create a f*cket and a funday list for the day. See "Create your f*cket and funday lists" on page 126 in chapter 5 "Self care".
Day 73	Declutter your living space.
Day 74	Complete a project you've been putting off.
Day 75	De-weed the garden. Baby will love being outside with you!
Day 76	Learn a new skill.
Day 77	Plan your next family outing or a special weekend getaway.

Get motivated with a certified life coach's productivity exercise to inspire you to take action. Visit our online course The Fourth Trimester Toolkit at WILDBEGINNINGS.THINKIFIC.COM, to learn more.

Week 12
Reflection and Planning

Day 78	Reflect on your postpartum journey.
Day 79	Celebrate your and baby's accomplishments.
Day 80	Book in a babysitter for a night off to reflect with your partner.
Day 81	Set personal goals for the upcoming months.
Day 82	Create a mood board for baby's first birthday.
Day 83	Write a letter to your future self for one year's time.
Day 84	Congratulations! You've survived your wild Fourth Trimester with your baby, celebrate by doing something you love!

Always remember, you are one WILD, #badass mumma!!!

Remember, this is just a guide, and it's important to listen to your intuition and your body and do what feels right for you.

Taking care of your mental health is crucial during the postpartum period, and it's important to seek professional help if needed.

Adjust the plan to fit your personal needs and preferences, and don't hesitate to ask for support if you need it.

CHAPTER
TEN
Other mummas' wild stories

Other mothers' stories

stories

Their wild beginnings in entering parenthood

Words from mummas who've been there...

EMMA'S STORY

"OUR FOURTH TRIMESTER WAS DURING THE PEAK OF SUMMER. I JUST REMEMBER IT BEING SUCH A BLUR OF CRAZY EMOTIONS."

Once our little boy was born, there were so many crazy emotions and hormones involved!

One minute I was completely exhausted; the next minute I got angry at stupid stuff. Like when my husband didn't cut a sandwich in half for me, so I couldn't eat it while I was breastfeeding. **I was also completely in love with my new little family and cried all the time at how fulfilled I felt.** I remember the overwhelming emotions.

It's obviously a massive learning curve. You're doing everything for the first time, and it all feels new. Bathing baby, bathing yourself, cooking dinner, breastfeeding, and even just leaving the house. You've got to accept that you're a beginner again - that's probably one of the hardest things.

I wish I knew that in the first three months everyone is winging it. There's a lot of advice thrown around when you're a new mum, especially with social media. I wish I trusted my gut a bit more and didn't overthink things or second-guess myself. I wish I knew that in the first three months everyone is winging it. Our boy is so happy and healthy and there's a million different ways to parent.

- Emma, Mum of Harley, Auckland, New Zealand.

REBECCA'S STORY

"NO ONE CAN PREPARE YOU FOR WHAT'S COMING. ONE CHALLENGE THAT STICKS OUT FOR ME IS THE PHYSICAL RELENTLESSNESS OF THAT TIME."

Once you're on the rollercoaster, you can't get off. Every three hours you're feeding, and you never really get that physical or mental break from it. No matter how helpful my husband was, I couldn't just go and have a complete break.

You're worried that if you go out and do something for yourself, the baby's going to get hungry while you are out of the house.

Everyone talks to you about how you should treasure those first few weeks with your little one because they'll pass so quickly. And I totally get that now. But at the time it was so hard. You've got so much else going on adjusting to your new life and you feel so isolated at the beginning. It's just you and the baby home for so long. **It's like you have no idea what you're doing and you're feeling all these things.**

During that newborn phase, babies are at their most vulnerable, plus you have no idea what you're doing. And you've got these crazy hormones. It's a kind of cruel moment in time that nature sets up for you.

For the first four or five weeks in the mid-afternoon, I started to feel this sense of impending doom.

It was like my life was over. Everything was just going to be hard forever. It would always be that time in the afternoon when this grey cloud would fill my mind.

I think feeding at that time almost made the feeling worse. And then as soon as the sun went down, I would be my happy self again. It was a tough combination of being tired towards the end of the day as well as the challenges of the day catching up on me.

When I got my head around the fact that it was consistently happening at that time of day and it was like an obvious pattern, it was more manageable.

At that time of the day, I was trying to do some yoga or some breathing.

Or I might have a cup of tea and some chocolate or reach out to my support network to help get through this tough time of the day.

I was lucky I had my husband off work for six weeks. But it was tough. My baby was very, very windy from about three weeks to eight weeks. So, he would scream after every feed. That was pretty hard going.

The other thing I found hard was that I'm a perfectionist. I've always been a person who works out how to do something or I'd read up on a topic and become an expert, trying my very best to be really good at something.

That was the hardest thing for me to get my head around. I wanted it to be like: if I do it like this, the baby will feel like this. But then he'd go through a week where he didn't want to nap and I would think what am I doing wrong? And I'd take the changes in routine very hard and beat myself up over it. Even though it's just life with a baby.

Drop your expectations of having a tidy house.

You can put a list of jobs that need doing around the house and stick it on your fridge so that when a visitor comes round they can see the list and pick one of the chores to do.

Why did we say goodbye to our old life and do this to ourselves?

I struggled with that. I remember looking at magazines in the early days and thinking, gosh, that person's had more than one child. It must be okay if that person had three. That was kind of my way of coping and thinking it must be okay if people do it more than once.

When his grandparents were getting delight from interacting with him, that gave me hope that it can't be all that bad. I ended up getting quite a bit of joy from seeing their joy.

From the six-week mark, things did get easier. And we got into more of a routine. I definitely feel like things have settled down and the other day I was thinking that he seems to be sleeping quite well.

– Rebecca, Mum of George, Auckland, New Zealand.

ANNALISE'S STORY

"AS SOON AS YOU GET HOME WITH A NEWBORN, YOU'RE SORT OF IN A STATE OF EUPHORIA. YOU'RE SO IN LOVE WITH THEM."

However, there were challenges.

My husband and I think that weeks two and three were the worst. Sleep deprivation is the biggest shock. We were fighting heaps and weren't ourselves at all. We're not really a couple that fights. But I told my midwife and she said, "you're sleep deprived; it's a form of torture."

We were sleeping in separate rooms and doing shifts - he's such an organised, doting dad.

Feeding was really difficult and I was in heaps of pain. I'd be crying or gritting my teeth with every latch. I have a chronic pain condition called fibromyalgia, so my back and my shoulders were all in spasm.

I was pumping and doing mixed feeding and then gradually went to just bottles. I got mastitis and then I fainted and had fevers. For me, it was worse than COVID.

When I made the decision to stop breastfeeding, everything changed.

And I've been loving it since. It was like a weight had lifted. And our son takes a bottle really well.

Denise Ives oversees an NGO called The Breast Room in Dunedin, New Zealand, and she counsels people with breastfeeding challenges. She came to my house once or twice a week, like a therapist.

I said to my midwife that I felt so guilty about stopping breastfeeding because of the pressure that you feel from society and the health system. But she was amazing and told me you've got to do what's best for you and your mental health.

I got diagnosed with postnatal depression.

As soon as you have the baby, it's like you're invisible. Everyone addresses the baby and talks to them, and you feel like you've been hit by a train.

For a time, my thoughts and feelings were so out of character, and I was in a deep depression. It was weird because I've always been a real motherly, bubbly extrovert.

I remember them skimming over mental health during the antenatal classes and because I'm a nurse I would ask: Where do we get information about that? I would try and get her to tell the girls where to go if they needed help.

Postnatal depression was a big shock and dealing with all the hormonal, physical, emotional, mental and relationship changes, too.

My advice is - don't have any expectations.

Put your mental health and your baby's health first. You've got to make sure that you're ready to face some huge challenges and changes and look after yourself in the process as well.

It takes a village.

For a lot of us, we don't have family close by or grandparents that are hands-on, so your village is your friends. Although they can't breastfeed for you, when they offer meals and other help, say yes. Accept all offers of help.

I felt like I had to entertain and make cups of tea for the grandparents. I think that they wait for your permission as the mum to pick up the baby but now they're getting more confident. So I ask them, "Can you please change his nappy for me?" Or "Can you do a bottle?" And they're learning and getting more confident too, so that's cool.

I've started a group with several girls of similar age, all first-time mums.

We all say it's been a lifeline having that community of mums. I guess it's not a surprise because I always wanted to be in the mum club. I'm really loving that aspect and girl power - women supporting women.

- Annalise, Mum of Alex,Dunedin, New Zealand.

TRINA'S STORY

"I'M AN EARLY CHILDHOOD TEACHER, SO WHILE I KNEW THE INS AND OUTS OF LOOKING AFTER A BABY, I WAS NOT PREPARED FOR THE OVERWHELMING MENTAL SWITCH OF BEING A NEW MUM."

There's so much reading you can do to prepare yourself for what's going to happen. I went to antenatal class. It's so cliche, but it didn't prepare me enough for what becoming a mum was going to be like.

I had quite a bit of anxiety in my third trimester and that carried on through the fourth trimester as well. I wasn't expecting to be as angry as much as I was. I didn't even know that was a perfectly normal reaction to becoming a mum. **There was a lot of grief as well that I really wasn't expecting.**

If I had that awareness that these emotions could be a possibility, I could have thought, okay, this is perfectly normal. Instead, I flipped into bouts of rage and thought, I'm not like this; this is really weird.

There was a little bit about postnatal depression discussed at my antenatal, but not really the depths that I needed it to be to help me handle what happened. I would love there to be more discussion and normalisation of those emotions.

In the early days, you see on the TV and the movies that it's all supposed to be happy. You cry because the baby's crying and you can't sleep, **but the media don't share the deeper range of emotions. I didn't have that awareness at all.**

Bonding issues

I remember saying to my husband while he was giving her a bath, "that's your job." I remember saying it's really weird because during the day I feel like I'm babysitting your child and then when you come home from work, you take over, and

I stop being a mum. It becomes your daughter after that. I just happen to be her carer.

It took a while to be able to share outside of my husband and my sister what was actually going on.

It was probably at least into week five or six postpartum that I reached out to another mum. I had awful trouble with bonding for a long time and I just quietly mentioned it to one of the other mums and she said, "I'm going through the same thing as well."

To hear another mum say, "me too" was a huge weight lifted off my shoulders. And for both of us, our bonding issues have improved over time.

For the people I've talked to so far, their bonding improved when their babies started to smile.

My daughter's first smile was the turning point for me, where I thought, I can do this. I'm not just looking after a random something. That's the part I had been looking forward to the most - the interaction of it.

Do what works for you and your baby

One time I ordered something and it arrived with a note, **"you are the exact mother your baby needs."**

I'd just been battling to get through every day and wondering when it was going to get any easier. So to read that note, I thought "I'm doing a great job in her eyes."

My advice to new mums is to trust your gut, take on the advice, but interpret it in your own way and do what works for you and your baby.

If I had trusted my instincts, I could have avoided some of the issues that I had. Instead of just taking everything that everyone says - you have to do this; you should do this; you can't ever do that - I wish I realised sooner that **not every baby's the same and everyone handles things differently.**

I think it was something that took me a long time to come to terms with, reading and listening to different people. Obviously they were the experts, but some of the stuff that was suggested - like feeding every three hours, which I took very literally - wasn't working and I just kept pushing through because I thought this is what I've been told. It's supposed to happen this way, so maybe she's broken or I'm broken. So I just kept pushing through.

Every new obstacle I approach, I'm trying to remind myself that all babies are different. If she doesn't do something by a certain age, then it's okay. Or if this works instead of that, then that's okay. And it's a lot of coming to terms with the fact that not everything's going to work for everyone.

If I do things my way, no one's going to come and tell me off or take her away. I'm the exact mother my daughter needs.

- Trina, Mum of Jasmine, Wellington, New Zealand.

A DOULA'S STORY

SHELLY MACKIE, POSTPARTUM DOULA

@thymeforyou_maternal_care

What are doulas and what do they do?

There are different kinds of doulas, I am a birth and postpartum doula.

Birth doulas support families in the transition to parenting through pregnancy, labour, birth, and the immediate postpartum period. We offer non-medical support that is informational, emotional, and physical in nature.

We can also translate medical jargon to help parents make informed decisions. As birth doulas, we are there to hold space for the people in the room, and that includes birthing partners and midwives. It's an absolute blessing to be there in this precious time.

As a postpartum doula, one of our roles is to "mother the mother". We wrap around the birthing family and support the birthing person so that they can rest and recover and have a blissful start into parenthood. We provide whānau (family) with information and support on various aspects of parenting such as coping skills, infant feeding and soothing. Other things we can do to help is light housework, help with other children and provide postpartum appropriate meals.

I'm also a massage therapist, reflexologist, and yoga teacher, so I put together some movement plans for mums, including some stretches for the shoulders and the hips. We can do nice relaxation exercises together. I also massage their feet. Other times, my role is to come over and clean the house or just listen and validate their experiences.

When did you become a doula?

I had quite a bit of trauma around the births of my own babies and felt that my body had failed, in my pursuit of understanding, I fell into the birthing world. I did a lot of self-reflection and healing along this journey into doulahood and completed my training in 2016.

Why is the Fourth Trimester such a precious time for the mum in particular?

In the Fourth Trimester, birthing people go through a very intense stage of neural development which is driven by hormones. Physiological structural changes occur in the brain and this postpartum brain has the same needs as a newborn brain.

Humans are a social species; this is what makes us so successful, and we need a village around us to support us. These days isolated nuclear families struggle because it's hard on our own. **We have lost the art of caring for new mums and families,** we don't know how to ask for or accept help and this can be isolating and very hard when you have a newborn. It's wonderful as a doula, to be able to meet some of those needs, by supporting parenting choices, addressing concerns and fears, helping them get rest and good quality nutrition.

The rates of postpartum mood disorders have been skyrocketing and we know that a supportive community can be a protective factor.

One of the most common questions as a new mum is "Is this normal? Is what I'm going through okay?" So, it's part of my job to reassure the mum that yes, this is normal. Yes, you're doing a fantastic job.

Essentially being a parent means you make mistake after mistake until you figure it out and then it changes.

That's why I think it's important that we ask: what are we doing to support the birthing people so that they can have a smooth transition into parenthood?

What about the difference between Eastern traditions and the Western way of looking after a mum?

Eastern traditions are interesting as they've come through the ages, through hundreds of years of traditions. In the old traditions a village or family wraps around the mum, cooking food. The new mum is in the presence of wise women. **We learn to mother by being around mothers.** Our sisters, friends and cousins would be having babies - there would be babies everywhere. We wouldn't second guess ourselves and question if what we're doing is normal and okay because we're surrounded by other mums and babies. We would help raise other people's babies too.

In New Zealand, a lot of those traditional practices have been lost due to colonisation. Māori and Pasifika cultures have got beautiful, deep traditions that are very beneficial for the new whānau.

I work from my instinct and my sacredness of being a mum. My work comes from a place of asking "what did I need when I was a new mum?"

If you ask any postpartum person what they need, its mostly FOOD! We get very hungry postpartum, and people come and see the baby, but they don't come and see the mum. **So, while we are holding and nurturing our babies, who's holding and nurturing us as parents?** And that's what is lost, the nurturing of the mum.

Once these women were career women, organisers, doers, they were Tanya and Sophie and Sue, and now they feel they're just the holder and provider for the baby. **In those first couple of months, you get this weird disassociation with who you were before and who you are now.**

Treating ourselves with compassion and love.

Having a baby changes your physiology, your body, your hormones, your brain, and your life.

It's very easy when you're tired to catastrophise. To think life will never be the same again; I'll never sleep again. Research shows us that a mother's cortisol level and her emotional state impact their baby's nervous system in utero. That's not to lay blame on mums but to highlight how important it is to nurture the mum through pregnancy and beyond.

I suffered from postpartum depression as well and it was undiagnosed. I went on to have my second child in a very emotionally unregulated state. I was full of rage, angst, and depression. I had a rough pregnancy with my son. My son does have some challenges and mum guilt is a huge thing.

Mum guilt is one of the most soul-destroying things. We are constantly berating ourselves for the things we haven't done or the way we've done things. We are so self-critical; **would you ever say the things that you say to yourself to your child?**

We wouldn't. So, changing that narrative one step at a time. When you catch yourself berating yourself, being mean to yourself, look at that wounded child inside of you.

If you looked at a mum with a newborn baby that was suffering as you did, would you judge her? No. You would just want to wrap her in love and compassion. **You deserve that same love and compassion.**

But because of all the work I've done, I can look back with compassion and say, "Why wasn't anyone there for me? Why was I left in that state for so long? Where was my support and why wasn't anyone holding me?"

Through that experience, I've been able to heal that mum guilt and support my son.

If we could support mums and change the narrative in pregnancy, birth and beyond, wouldn't we have a much more peaceful world? Healing the world one birth, one mother at a time.

And what do you find is the most rewarding thing about your job?

As a birth doula, my favourite moments are when the baby has just been born and the birth giver is holding the baby with such tenderness and adoration and the birthing partner is just looking at them in awe, love, and reverence. They are holding the baby and after all that work, they think, "Here you are" and just so in love with their baby, and that moment is magical, sacred, and beautiful.

In the postpartum period, when a mum and family come into their own as parents and you see that shift and click of knowing. Mumma bear comes out and you see that sovereign authority that is inside of us.

When we have children, a lot of people find their inner lioness and that's one of the most magnificent things I've ever seen.

I think the bravery that parents show is just incredible - it gives me goosebumps. When you see parents in antenatal classes, they're all excited and there's lots of joking and uncertainness. Then they come out the other side and the mask is ripped off. It's so raw; so beautiful.

What would you like mums that are in their Third Trimester to know about what's coming up?

Be informed of all your rights and choices, be soft, be open to surrender, your birth team -including your Lead Maternity Carer (LMC) – need to have the same birthing ethos as you.

You can do all the birth planning in the world, but you don't know what's going to happen on the day.

Plan for postpartum - build your village, your sacred circle wisely with discernment. Ask for and accept help. Asking for help not only benefits you, but it teaches and empowers others to step up for you and other postpartum whānau.

If we don't ask for help, people don't know how to look after us. If we don't accept help, we are not loving and respecting the people that want to come and help us because every one of us would like to do service for the people we love. Every one of us wants to be there. We want that person in our life to feel loved.

What I would like to say to postpartum mums is when people show up, particularly those that haven't had babies, tell them what you need so they feel they have value to you. Then when they go to visit another postpartum person, they can do the same for that whānau (family).

This way we will be changing how society looks after people one birth at a time.

> We live in a patriarchal world which is focused on doing, achieving and results. We're not taught how to watch, see and to hold. But that's how we parent - by watching for the cues and reading between the lines.

It's a real skill to be able to hold space for people and not jump straight into problem-solving mode. We've been trained in masculine skills, but not feminine skills. But it's those feminine skills that are needed during birth and the postpartum period, so mums are seen and heard. Those skills help mothers feel validated and visible - they are acknowledged that what they're doing is valuable.

Can you tell me about one of the mums you supported.

One new mum was an immigrant, and she didn't have any family here. Unfortunately, she couldn't have a village. But she did have me, her partner, and her midwife.

Their baby was born in September which meant I couldn't attend the birth because we were in covid lockdown. However, her midwife wrote a letter to give me permission to be her care provider.

I brought her food twice a week so I could fill her fridge and freezer with food that would carry her through - overnight oats, nuts, and easy snacks. Chicken, soups and stews, and wholefood muffins.

Every time I visited, we spoke about her fears and questions, and I gave her evidence-based research that I found. I gave her a back and shoulder massage at each visit and taught her how to position herself during breastfeeding to alleviate neck and shoulder tension as well as help with a fast flow and a windy baby, I also assisted her learning how to get a deep latch as she was experiencing blistering.

She spent the first four weeks in bed with her baby skin-to-skin bonding. Occasionally she would go for a walk in the beautiful park nearby. By week three she had spent so much time with her baby, that her oxytocin levels - the love hormone - were really heightened. She was also getting great rest and nutrition.

She was so connected to her baby that when her baby was three weeks old, mum knew when they were going to wee or poo so she would put the baby on the potty - a technique called Elimination Communication, - now that's an extreme example. But even now, their baby is nine months old, and she is such a confident, calm and in-tune māmā. I put that down to spending that amazing amount of time with her baby and building up as much oxytocin as possible.

Her partner took extended time off work.

When mum was feeling overwhelmed and touched out, he would wear the baby and go for a walk for an hour. He also asked for help from his family and friends and the wider community, and they set up a meal train. He was very involved as a parent and did a lot of research, so they had this great pool of information that they managed to put together.

What do you love most about being a mum?

Watching my children discover who they are. It's been an amazing journey. And I also think it's made me a far wiser, braver, more compassionate, and patient person.

I'm hoping the more we educate people, the ripples will go further, and we can transform how people are raising children and looking after mums and families. Responding to a birthing person's needs helps them become responsive attuned parents and this is protective to both of their brilliant brains in this sensitive period.

Where can mums learn more about your services?

Thyme For You Perinatal Care on Facebook and Instagram (@ thymeforyou_maternal_care)

- Shelly Mackie, Mum of Shayle & Erin, Christchurch, New Zealand.

Resources

AVOID THE EARLY MORNING GOOGLING!

I hope these resources will be helpful. However, please note these websites are subject to change.

From Pip Findlay, Founder of Wild Beginnings

- Wild Beginnings online courses: **https://wildbeginnings.thinkific.com/**
- Wild Beginnings on Instagram: **https://www.instagram.com/wildbeginningsnz/**
- Wild Beginnings on Facebook: **https://www.facebook.com/wildbeginningsnz/**
- Read my article "Entering the Wild World of Parenthood" for tips and guidance for new parents here. **https://parentscentre.org.nz/information/entering-the-wild-world-of-parenthood/**

Services and Support during Pregnancy

- Services and Support During Pregnancy - New Zealand Ministry of Health. This website provides information on healthcare services available during pregnancy, childbirth, and postpartum period in New Zealand. **https://www.health.govt.nz/your-health/pregnancy-and-kids/services-and-support-during-pregnancy**
- Advanced Women's Health - Dr. Sarah Wilson, ND: Dr. Sarah Wilson is a Naturopathic Doctor specializing in women's health. Her website provides information on various women's health topics, including hormones during fertility, pregnancy, and postpartum. **https://www.advancedwomenshealth.ca/dr-sarah-wilson-nd**

- Dr. Sarah Wilson, ND on Instagram. **https://www.instagram.com/drsarah_nd/**
- LGBTQI+ Pathway – Fertility Associates New Zealand: This website provides information on fertility options for the LGBTQI+ community in New Zealand. **https://www.fertilityassociates.co.nz/pathway/lgbttqiplus/**
- LGBTQ+ Options – Fertility New Zealand: This website provides information on fertility options for the LGBTQ+ community in New Zealand. **https://www.fertilitynz.org.nz/information/donation-and-other-options/lgbtq/**
- Find Your Midwife: This website helps new mums find a midwife in New Zealand. It provides a directory of midwives in different regions of the country. **https://www.findyourmidwife.co.nz/**
- New Zealand Doula Association: This website provides information on doula services in New Zealand, including a directory of doulas in different regions of the country. **https://www.nzdoulas.nz/**

Postpartum Education

- Adjusting to Life with a Baby – Plunket: This webpage provides information on how to adjust to life with a new baby, including tips on bonding, feeding, and sleep. **https://www.plunket.org.nz/being-a-parent/looking-after-you/health-and-care-after-birth/adjusting-to-life-with-a-baby/**
- Baby Sleep Tips – Plunket on YouTube: This video provides tips on how to help your baby sleep better. **https://www.youtube.com/watch?v=WjOowWxOXCg&t=6s**
- Getting Enough Sleep – Plunket: This webpage provides tips on how new parents can get enough sleep, even with a newborn. **https://www.plunket.org.nz/being-a-parent/looking-after-you/health-and-care-after-birth/getting-enough-sleep/**

- Your Body After Birth - Plunket: This webpage provides information on the physical changes new mums can expect after giving birth, and tips on how to take care of themselves during recovery. **https://www.plunket.org.nz/being-a-parent/looking-after-you/health-and-care-after-birth/your-body-after-birth/**
- Advanced Women's Health - Dr. Sarah Wilson, ND: Dr. Sarah Wilson's website provides information on various women's health topics, including fertility, pregnancy, and postpartum care. **https://www.advancedwomenshealth.ca/dr-sarah-wilson-nd**

Mental Health

- Perinatal Anxiety and Depression Aotearoa (PADA): PADA provides information and support for those experiencing antenatal and postnatal depression and anxiety. **https://pada.nz/**
- Mothers Helpers: Mothers Helpers provides counselling and support for mothers experiencing postnatal depression and anxiety. **https://www.mothershelpers.co.nz/pnd/**
- Parent Mental Health - Plunket: This webpage provides information on how to take care of your mental health as a new parent, including tips on coping with stress and seeking help if needed. **https://www.plunket.org.nz/being-a-parent/looking-after-you/parent-mental-health/**
- Mothers Matter: This website provides resources and support for mothers experiencing postnatal depression and anxiety. **https://www.mothersmatter.nz/**
- Postnatal Distress Support Network: This website provides support and resources for those experiencing postnatal depression and anxiety. **https://postnataldistress.co.nz/**

- Mental Health Foundation of New Zealand: The Mental Health Foundation provides information and resources for those experiencing mental health challenges, including postnatal depression and anxiety. **https://mentalhealth.org.nz/**

Trauma and Childbirth

- Trauma and Birth Stress (TABS): TABS provides support and resources for those who have experienced trauma during childbirth, including post-traumatic stress disorder (PTSD). **http://www.tabs.org.nz/index.htm**
- Advocacy for Mothers and Babies: This organization provides advocacy and support for mothers and babies, including those who have experienced trauma during childbirth. **https://advocacy.org.nz/**
- My Birth Story: This website allows new mothers to share their birth stories and connect with others who have had similar experiences. **https://www.mybirthstory.org.nz/what-is-it**

Feeding Support

- Breastfeeding School: This online course provides information and resources for new mothers who want to learn more about breastfeeding by Jana Stockham, an Internationally Certified Lactation Consultant and Registered Nurse who has helped thousands of mums. **https://breastfeeding.teachable.com/**
- You can also learn from Jana via Pip's online course The Fourth Trimester Toolkit at **https://wildbeginnings.thinkific.com/courses/FourthTrimester.**
- Huggies: This webpage provides information and tips on breastfeeding and bottle-feeding. **https://www.huggies.co.nz/baby-care/breasteeding-and-bottle-feeding**

- KellyMom: KellyMom is a website that provides evidence-based information and resources on breastfeeding. **https://kellymom.com/category/bf/**
- Breastfeeding-Friendly Workplaces - Women's Health Action: This webpage provides information and resources for employers and employees on creating breastfeeding-friendly workplaces. **https://www.womens-health.org.nz/breastfeeding-friendly-workplaces/**
- Crying Over Spilt Milk: This website provides information and support for mothers who are experiencing breastfeeding challenges. **https://www.cryingoverspiltmilk.co.nz/**
- Mamma's Milk Bar: This website provides information on safe protein powder options and lactation blends for pregnant and breastfeeding mothers. **https://mammasmilkbar.com/pages/safe-protein-powder-pregnancy**

Pelvic Floor Health

- Unity Studios: Unity Studios is a New Zealand-based physiotherapy clinic that specializes in pelvic health and postpartum rehabilitation. **https://unitystudios.co.nz/**
- Unity Studios Blog: Unity Studios also maintains a blog that provides informative articles and resources on postpartum recovery and pelvic health. **https://unitystudios.co.nz/blog/**
- Sophie Lax Physio: This Instagram account is run by a New Zealand-based physiotherapist who specializes in pelvic health, postpartum recovery, and sports injury rehabilitation. **https://www.instagram.com/sophielaxphysio/**
- You can learn from Sophie in Pip's online course The Fourth Trimester Toolkit at **https://wildbeginnings.thinkific.com/courses/FourthTrimester.**

- The Vagina Physio: This Instagram account is run by a New Zealand-based physiotherapist who specializes in pelvic health and postpartum recovery. **https://www.instagram.com/ thevaginaphysio/?hl=en**
- Continence Foundation of New Zealand: This website provides information and resources on pelvic health and continence, including postpartum recovery. **https://www.continence.org.nz/ pages/One-in-three-woman-who-ever-had-a-baby-wet-themselves/38/**
- ACC Maternal Birth Injuries: The New Zealand Accident Compensation Corporation (ACC) provides information and resources for healthcare providers on maternal birth injuries. **https://www.acc.co.nz/for-providers/maternal-birth-injuries/**

Postnatal Nutrition

- The Natal Nutritionist Instagram: This Instagram account is run by the Natal Nutritionist and provides informative resources on prenatal and postnatal nutrition. **https://www.instagram.com/ thenatalnutritionist/**
- You can learn from Amanda, The natal nutritionist, in Pip's online course The Fourth Trimester Toolkit at **https://wildbeginnings. thinkific.com/courses/FourthTrimester.**
- Parents Centre New Zealand: This website provides a wide range of resources for parents, including prenatal and postnatal education, support, and advocacy. This article covers postnatal nutrient depletion and how to maintain optimal nutrition postpartum. **https://parentscentre.org.nz/information/ preventing-postnatal-nutrient-depletion/**
- Soteria: Soteria is a New Zealand-based wellness centre that provides postpartum nutrition advice and support. **https:// soteria.co.nz/health-wellbeing/postpartum-nutrition-advice/**

- Auckland Family Nutrition: This website provides information and resources on postnatal nutrition, including meal planning and nutrient requirements. **https://aucklandfamilynutrition.co.nz/ postnatal-nutrition/**

Financial Planning

- Plunket New Zealand: Planning your finances for a new baby. **https://www.plunket.org.nz/being-a-parent/preparing-for-your-baby/work-and-financial-planning/planning-your-finances/**
- Money and You New Zealand: How to financially prepare for parenthood. **https://www.moneyandyou.org.nz/blog/how-to-financially-prepare-for-parenthood**
- Sorted New Zealand: Planning for a family. **https://sorted.org.nz/ guides/planning-and-budgeting/planning-for-a-family**

Self-care for New Mums

- Me and My Child: Post-Baby Self Care Tips. **https://www. meandmychild.co.nz/parenting-support/post-baby-self-care-tips**
- Haakaa: Postpartum Self Care. **https://www.haakaa.co.nz/ blogs/blog/postpartum-self-care**
- Health Navigator NZ: Mental wellbeing for new mums. **https:// www.healthnavigator.org.nz/healthy-living/m/mental-wellbeing-for-new-mums/**

Social Life & Relationships

- Plunket: Social life and relationships. **https://www.plunket. org.nz/being-a-parent/looking-after-you/social-life-and-relationships/**

- The 5 Love Languages - Learn the 5 Love Languages. **https://www.5lovelanguages.com/learn/**
- Cassandra Hogan, certified life coach and Founder of Fontein Coaching: Blog. **https://www.fonteincoaching.co.nz/blog**
- You can learn more from Cassandra in Pip's online course The Fourth Trimester Toolkit at **https://wildbeginnings.thinkific.com/courses/FourthTrimester.**

Support for Fathers

- Plunket New Zealand - Adjusting to life with a baby. **https://www.plunket.org.nz/being-a-parent/looking-after-you/health-and-care-after-birth/adjusting-to-life-with-a-baby/#adjusting-to-being-a-dad**

Support for Parents of Premature Babies

- Little Miracles - Supporting families with premature or sick babies. **https://littlemiraclestrust.org.nz/**

Support for single mothers

- Mothers Helpers - Support for single parents. **https://www.mothershelpers.co.nz/single-parents/**
- Single Parent Support - Support for single parents in New Zealand. **http://spsw.org.nz/**

Support for Multiples

- CareforKids: Support Available to Parents of Multiples. **https://www.careforkids.co.nz/child-care-articles/article/360/support-available-to-parents-of-multiples**
- Multiple Births Foundation: Support for Parents of Multiples. **https://www.multiplebirths.org.uk/**

Support for going back to work

- Women's Health: Breastfeeding-Friendly Workplaces. **https:// www.womens-health.org.nz/breastfeeding-friendly- workplaces/**
- Plunket: Returning to Work. **https://www.plunket.org.nz/being-a- parent/looking-after-you/returning-to-work/**

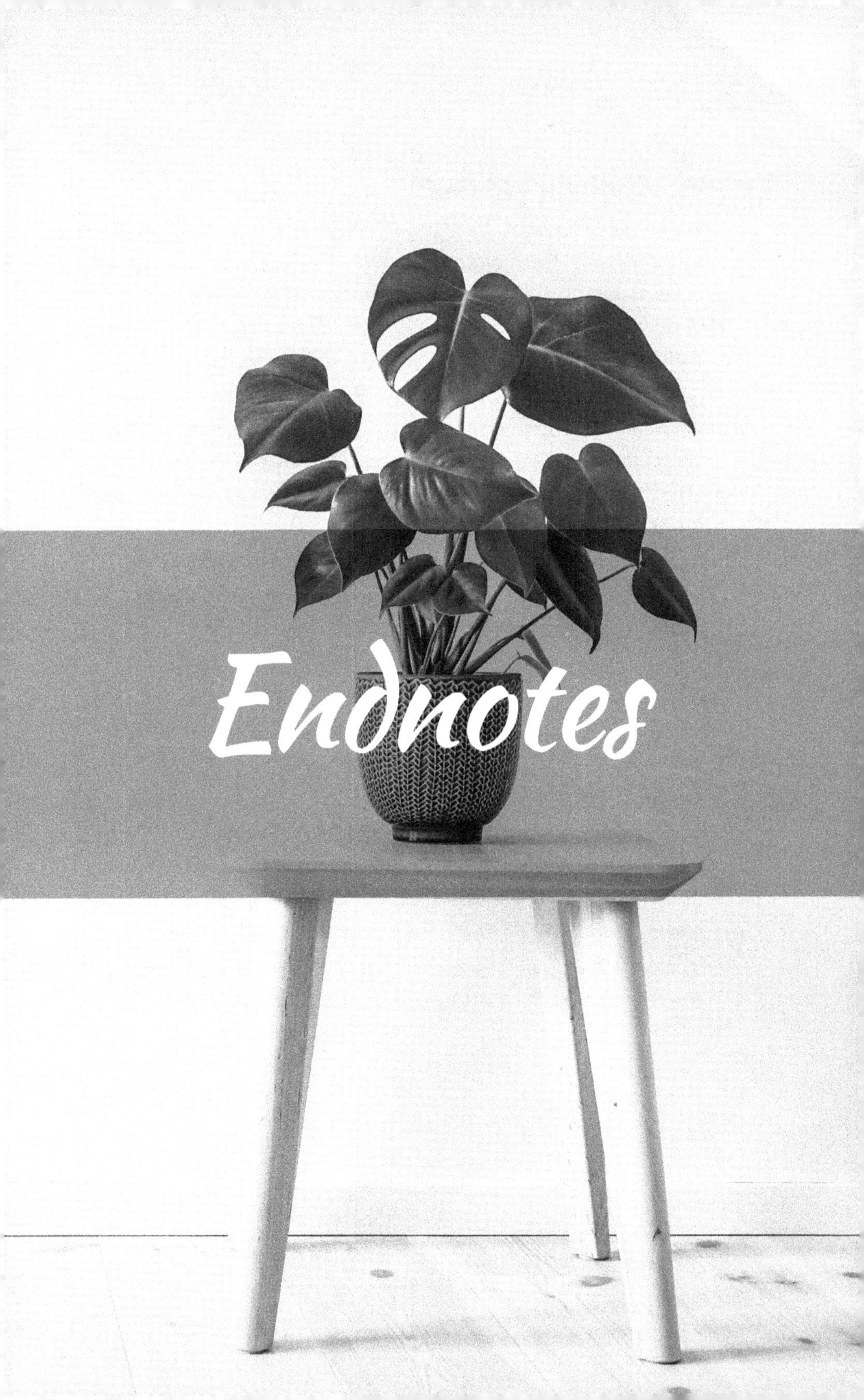
Endnotes

Chapter 1: Your Postpartum.

- Richter, D., Krämer, M., Tang, N., Montgomery-Downs, H., & Lemola, S. (2019). *Long-term effects of pregnancy and childbirth on sleep satisfaction and duration of first-time and experienced mothers and fathers.* Sleep, 42(5), zsz015. **https://doi.org/10.1093/sleep/zsz015**

- Pacheco, D. (2023, February 7). *How Does Being a New Parent Affect Sleep?* Retrieved from **https://www.sleepfoundation.org/sleep-deprivation/parents#:~:text=Parents'%20sleep%20often%20does%20not,%2Drefreshing%20sleep%2C%20and%20fatigue**.

- MedlinePlus. (2017, April 26*). Healthy Sleep. Also called: Sleep Hygiene*. Retrieved from **https://medlineplus.gov/healthysleep.html**.

- Frost, A. (2022, March 14). *Everything you need to know about your post-pregnancy belly.* Retrieved from **https://www.babycenter.com/baby/postpartum-health/post-baby-belly-how-long-you-might-look-pregnant_1152349**.

- Sparks, D. (2017, August 3). *Women's Wellness: Breastfeeding and weight loss.* Retrieved from **https://www.mayoclinic.org/healthy-lifestyle/labor-and-delivery/in-depth/weight-loss-after-pregnancy/art-20047813#:~:text=Most%20women%20lose%20about%2013,t%20disappear%20on%20its%20own**.

- Mackie, S. (2022, July 5). Founder of Thyme for You Perinatal Care. *The Five Pillars of Postpartum*. Interviewed in July 2022.

Chapter 2: Hooray for Hormones!

- Dr Wilson, ND, S. (2021, Oct 25)- Founder of Advanced Women Health, interviewed in October 2021.

- Dr A Zenhausern (22 July 2020). *Your Postpartum Hormone Timeline: Here's What Happens.* Retrieved from **https://hellopostpartum.com/postpartum-hormone-timeline/**

- Author and date unknown. It's Bodily.com. *Birth Recovery & Postpartum Timeline.* Retrieved on 22 March 2022 from **https://itsbodily.com/pages/postpartum-recovery-time-timeline?sscid=31k6_nwcb5&utm_source=affiliate&utm_medium=shareasale&utm_campaign=1665296**

- Author Unknown (28 Feb 2018). *What to Expect from Your First Period After Pregnancy.* Retrieved from **https://www.healthline.com/health/pregnancy/first-period-postpartum#1**

- J Sacher, A A Wilson, S Houle, P Rusjan, S Hassan, P M Bloomfield, D E Stewart, J H Meyer (May 2010). *Elevated Brain Monoamine Oxidase A Binding in the Early Postpartum Period.* Retrieved from **https://doi.org/10.1001/archgenpsychiatry.2010.32**

- Anxiety and Depression Association of America (Date Unknown). *Postpartum Depression & Anxiety.* Retrieved on 22 March 2022 from **https://adaa.org/sites/default/files/adaa-psi-infogr_31503384%20(1).pdf**

- Postpartum Support International (PSI). (Date Unknown*). Postpartum Post-traumatic Stress Disorder.* Retrieved on 22 March 2022 from **https://www.postpartum.net/learn-more/postpartum-post-traumatic-stress-disorder/**

- Anxiety and Depression Association of America (Date Unknown). *Postpartum Disorders.* Retrieved on 22 March 2022 from **https://adaa.org/find-help-for/women/postpartum-disorders**

- National Institute of Mental Health, USA. (Date Unknown). *Perinatal Depression.* Retrieved on 22 March 2022 from **https://www.nimh.nih.gov/health/publications/perinatal-depression**

- Bodily. (n.d.). *Postpartum Emotions & Changes After Giving Birth.* Retrieved from **https://itsbodily.com/blogs/birth-recovery-postpartum/postpartum-emotions-changes-after-giving-birth**.
- Flo. (n.d.). *Hormones After Birth.* Retrieved from **https://flo.health/being-a-mom/recovering-from-birth/postpartum-problems/hormones-after-birth**.
- Today's Parent. (2018, February 22). *Mind-blowing ways your body changes after giving birth.* Retrieved from **https://www.todaysparent.com/baby/postpartum-care/mind-blowing-ways-your-body-changes-after-giving-birth/**.
- Verywell Family. (2021, August 18). *What Is Mom Brain?* Retrieved from **https://www.verywellfamily.com/what-is-mom-brain-4774384**.
- BBC News. (2016, December 14). *Pregnancy 'resculpts women's brains for at least two years'.* Retrieved from **https://www.bbc.com/news/health-38341901**.
- Hoekzema, E., Barba-Müller, E., Pozzobon, C., Picado, M., Lucco, F., García-García, D., … Carmona, S. (2016). *Pregnancy leads to long-lasting changes in human brain structure.* Nature Neuroscience, 20(2), 287–296. **https://doi.org/10.1038/nn.4458**
- HealthTimes. (2016, July 6). *Australian study shows "baby brain" does exist.* Retrieved from **https://healthtimes.com.au/hub/midwifery/38/news/aap/australian-study-shows-baby-brain-does-exist/3113/**.
- Peachymama. (n.d.). *Is Mumnesia A Thing?* Retrieved from **https://www.peachymama.com.au/blogs/motherhood/is-mumnesia-a-thing**.
- Healthline. (2020, June 23). *How Pregnancy Changes the Brain: Gray Matter, Connectivity, and Permeability.* Retrieved from **https://www.healthline.com/health-news/pregnancy-effects-on-brain#Changes-in-the-brain**.

- MadeForMums. (2019, April 2). *Are you suffering from "mumnesia"?* Retrieved from **https://www.madeformums.com/baby/are-you-suffering-from-mumnesia/**.
- Optimal Living Dynamics. "25 Effective Ways to Increase Oxytocin Levels in the Brain." Accessed on 21 June 2022. Retrieved from **https://www.optimallivingdynamics.com/blog/25-effective-ways-to-increase-oxytocin-levels-in-the-brain.**

Chapter 3: Confronting unspoken experiences. Tackling the Taboo Topics of Motherhood.

- WebMD. (2021, April 14). *Forming a Bond With Your Baby: Why It Isn't Always Immediate.* Retrieved from **https://www.webmd.com/parenting/baby/forming-a-bond-with-your-baby-why-it-isnt-always-immediate#1**
- Sacks, A. & Birndorf, C. (2019). *What No One Tells You: A Guide to Your Emotions from Pregnancy to Motherhood.* New York: Simon & Schuster.
- Sacks, A. *A New Way to Think About the Transition to Motherhood.* TED video, 12:02. Filmed September 2018. Posted October 2018. **https://www.ted.com/talks/alexandra_sacks_a_new_way_to_think_about_the_transition_to_motherhood?language=en**.
- "Maternal Instinct is a Myth That Endangers Mums and Babies." Stuff. Accessed on 15 April 2021. Retrieved from **https://www.stuff.co.nz/life-style/parenting/124808921/maternal-instinct-is-a-myth-that-endangers-mums-and-babies?cid=app-android&fbclid=IwAR2HExDZbTnLCaQdvkDyuXoQVvggrcBujbhgGQe5aqfSt4680bfO7FFtDNA.**
- Breastfeed LA: The Breastfeeding Task Force of Greater Los Angeles. Facebook (2019, 18 Nov). Accessed on 30 July 2021. Retrieved from **https://www.facebook.com/BreastfeedLA/photos/in-a-zoo-in-ohio-a-female-gorilla-was-born-and-**

raised-in-captivity-got-pregnant-/2556713934382316/?pa
ipv=0&eav=AfZd_8r3-zIWV7q5e22I7c4srpOV6gFHAO-
XRXnhKAB0wO1RV6zG-KwVtA_PciFD5N54&_rdr

- Crystal renee cooper. "Super-natural breastfeeding: how lactation consultants in hawai'i demedicalize and reshape women's embodied experiences." Publisher/Organization. Accessed on 21 May 2023. Retrieved from **https://scholarspace. manoa.hawaii.edu/server/api/core/bitstreams/f5dfc44b-c340-46d6-b469-4856c34e39d7/content**

Chapter 4: Your Matrescence.

- Romper. (n.d.). *Resenting Your Partner After Baby? Why It's Normal & What To Do About It.* Retrieved from **https://www. romper.com/pregnancy/resenting-your-partner-after-baby-why**
- Kirby, J. (2019, July 12). *Grieving Your Past Life When Becoming a Mom.* Retrieved from **https://www.jessannkirby.com/grieving-your-past-life-when-becoming-a-mom/**
- Sacks, A. & Birndorf, C. (2019). *What No One Tells You: A Guide to Your Emotions from Pregnancy to Motherhood.* New York: Simon & Schuster.
- Sacks, A. *A New Way to Think About the Transition to Motherhood.* TED video, 12:02. Filmed September 2018. Posted October 2018. **https://www.ted.com/talks/alexandra_sacks_a_new_way_to_think_about_the_transition_to_motherhood?language=en**.

Chapter 5: Self-care Strategies & Tips.

- Bounty Parents. (n.d.). *Self-care is important for new mums.* Retrieved from **https://www.bountyparents.com.au/expert-advice/self-care-important-for-new-mums/**

- Annabel Karmel. (n.d.). *New Mum F**ket List.* Retrieved from **https://www.annabelkarmel.com/advice/new-mum-fcket-list/**
- What to Expect. (n.d.). *10 Self-Care Ideas for New Moms.* Retrieved from **https://www.whattoexpect.com/first-year/you-and-your-health/self-care-ideas-moms**
- Empower Mums. (n.d.). *8 Self Care Ideas When You Are A Busy Mum.* Retrieved from **https://www.empowermums.co.nz/post/8-self-care-ideas-when-you-are-a-busy-mum**
- Clements, C. (2022, August). Founder of Olive & Pop. *An Entrepreneurial Mumma's Mantra & her Top 20 Tips.* Interviewed in August 2022.

Chapter 6: Nourishing your Baby - Your Way.

- Poon, W. (2022, August). Founder of Mammas Milk Bar. *Wendy's Wise Words.* Interviewed in August 2022.
- USDA. (n.d.). *How much milk your baby needs.* Retrieved from **https://wicbreastfeeding.fns.usda.gov/how-much-milk-your-baby-needs#:~:text=At%20birth%2C%20your%20baby's%20tummy,much%20milk%20your%20baby%20needs**.
- NHS. (n.d.). *Cluster feeding.* Retrieved from **https://www.nhs.uk/start4life/baby/feeding-your-baby/bottle-feeding/how-to-bottle-feed/cluster-feeding/#:~:text=Cluster%20feeding%20usually%20happens%20during,or%20a%20bit%20of%20both**)
- Simply Breastfeeding. (n.d.). *Simply Breastfeeding.* Retrieved from **https://www.simplybreastfeeding.ca/p/simply-breastfeeding**
- Stockham, J. (April 2020). *How To Breastfeeding Videos.* Retrieved from **https://wildbeginnings.thinkific.com/order?ct=f30dda1d-f8e0-416d-ab09-f2cb812bed0e**
- Mamma's Milk Bar. *Safe Protein Powder During Pregnancy.* Accessed April 22, 2023. **https://mammasmilkbar.com/pages/**

safe-protein-powder-pregnancy.

- Huggies New Zealand. *Breastfeeding and Bottle Feeding.* Retrieved from **https://www.huggies.co.nz/baby-care/ breasteeding-and-bottle-feeding**.

Chapter 7: Postpartum Nutrition.

- Bodily. (n.d.). *Postpartum Constipation: How Long, Hydration, and More.* Retrieved from **https://itsbodily.com/blogs/birth-recovery-postpartum/postpartum-constipation-how-long-hydration**
- Bodily. (n.d.). *Postpartum Hemorrhoids: Treatment, Bleeding, and More.* Retrieved from **https://itsbodily.com/blogs/birth-recovery-postpartum/postpartum-hemorrhoids-treatment-bleeding**
- Bennett, A (2021, April). Founder of The Neonatal Nutritionist. *Postpartum Nutrition.* Interviewed in April 2021.
- Plunket New Zealand. (n.d.). *Looking After Yourself When Breastfeeding: Eating Well.* Retrieved from **https://www.plunket. org.nz/caring-for-your-child/feeding/breastfeeding/looking-after-yourself-when-breastfeeding/#eating-well**.

Chapter 8: Pelvic Health & Exercise.

- Fogarty, S (2021, March). Co-founder of Unity Studios. *Pelvic Health & Safely returning to Exercise.* Interviewed in March 2021.
- Unity Studios. (n.d.). *Myth Busting: Caesarean Section Recovery Takes Longer Than Vaginal Delivery.* Retrieved from **https:// unitystudios.co.nz/myth-busting-caesarean-section-recovery-takes-longer-than-vaginal-delivery/**.
- Mum Bub Hub. (n.d.). *DIY Padsicles: How To Make Your Own Cold Pack for Pain Relief After Birth.* Retrieved from **https:// mumbubhub.com.au/diy-padsicles/**
- Unity Studios. *Returning to Running After Childbirth.* Retrieved from

https://unitystudios.co.nz/returning-to-running-after-childbirth/.

- Unity Studios. *Diastasis of Rectus Abdominis Muscle (Diastasis Recti, Rectus Abdominis Diastasis, Separation of the Abdominal Muscles).* Retrieved from **https://unitystudios.co.nz/diastasis-of-rectus-abdominis-muscle-diastasis-recti-rectus-abdominis-diastasis-seperation-of-the-abdominal-muscles/**.

- Unity Studios. *When to See a Pelvic Floor Physio.* Retrieved from **https://unitystudios.co.nz/when-to-see-a-pelvic-floor-physio/**.

- Unity Studios. *An Interesting Study on Painful Sex After Childbirth.* Retrieved from **https://unitystudios.co.nz/an-interesting-study-on-painful-sex-after-childbirth/**.

- Unity Studios. *Returning to Sex After Childbirth.* Retrieved from **https://unitystudios.co.nz/returning-to-sex-after-childbirth/**.

- Unity Studios. *Things to Help You Recover After a Caesarian.* Retrieved from **https://unitystudios.co.nz/things-to-help-you-recover-after-a-ceasarian/**.

- Unity Studios. *To Poo or Not to Poo and How to Do It Right.* Retrieved from **https://unitystudios.co.nz/to-poo-or-not-to-poo-and-how-to-do-it-right/**.

- Unity Studios. *Painful Sex.* Retrieved from **https://unitystudios.co.nz/painful-sex/**.

- ACC. Maternal Birth Injuries. Retrieved from **https://www.acc.co.nz/for-providers/maternal-birth-injuries/**.

- Continence New Zealand. *One in Three Women Who Ever Had a Baby Wet Themselves.* Retrieved from **https://www.continence.org.nz/pages/One-in-three-women-who-ever-had-a-baby-wet-themselves/38/**.

Chapter 9: A Plan to Thrive

- Findlay, P. (2023, April 22). Wild Beginnings. *Daily 12 Week Plan to Thrive in Postpartum. Compiled with the support and information received from the experts on the Fourth Trimester Toolkit panel at* **wildbeginnings.thinkific.com.**

Chapter 10: Other Mummas' Wild Stories

- Emma Mak. Whatsapp Voice note recording. June 2022.
- Annalise Appleby. Interview by Katie Rickson. Personal Interview. July 2022, Zoom Interview.
- Trina Edward-Paul. Interview by Katie Rickson. Personal Interview. July 2022, Zoom Interview.
- Rebecca McPhee. Interview by Katie Rickson. Personal Interview. July 2022, Zoom Interview.
- Shelly Mackie. Interview by Katie Rickson. Personal Interview. July 2022, Zoom Interview.

Acknowledgements

I want to express my deepest gratitude to all those who have supported me throughout the creation of this book.

Firstly, a huge thank you to my copywriters Katie Rickson and Kath Speller for your tireless work in helping to shape my words into a cohesive whole. Your contribution is invaluable, and no one quite knows how to wordsmith words like you two do! Thank you.

I want to thank my midwives. To Jo Mendoza, for being there for the birth of both my children, Harrison and Taylor. And to my closest friend, Kayleigh Jeevaratnam, who not only helped me birth (laugh!) Taylor into the world but also gave into my demand for an epidural. Thank you both for your guidance and care during my pregnancies, births, and early postpartum journeys. Your kindness, knowledge and expertise made all the difference. You provided me with the support and encouragement I needed during those early days of motherhood, and I am so grateful for your dedication and commitment to helping new mothers everywhere navigate this wild journey.

To my close friend and fellow Parents Centre Aotearoa Educator and Doula, Shelly Mackie, thank you for sharing your wisdom and experience with me. I have learned so much from you and your guidance has been instrumental in shaping this book and supporting me along my path in educating new mummas and running online and in-person workshops. And of course, thank you to the team at Parents Centre Aotearoa for providing me with the opportunity to educate many, many mummas and families in my time teaching the Being a Parent nationwide classes, and the All About You in-person workshops. I've been so fortunate to work with so many new, beautiful mummas and babes!

To my dear friends and fellow mothers, Annalise Appleby, Emma Mak, Rebecca McPhee, and Trina Edward-Paul, thank you for sharing your personal stories with me and with other mums who may be struggling, for opening up to the world essentially. Your honesty, vulnerability, and resilience are an inspiration, and I am honoured to know you.

Thank you to the wonderful women and experts in the parenthood field I've managed to meet along the way. To Internationally Certified Lactation Consultant and Registered Nurse, Jana Stockham, behind New Mom Collective, for all your valuable videos on breastfeeding and supporting mothers in any which way they choose to feed their babies. To Heidi Hadley of Total Somatics, whose unwavering encouragement for me to educate and support new mums has helped bring this to life. To my friend and incredible practitioner who helped improve my pelvic floor situation after birth, Senior Pelvic Floor Therapist and Co-founder of Unity Studios, Sophie Fogarty, as well as to The Vagina Physio, Caitlin Day, who also gave me a new lease on my sex life following birth (which at the time I never would have thought possible!) - thank you! Also to the lovely Nutritionist, Amanda Bennet, for being so generous and supportive in this project. To Dr. Sarah Wilson, ND, for teaching me all about postpartum hormones and helping to unpack the fact that I wasn't just a crazy lady for the couple of years following birth. To my friend and amazing entrepreneur of the lactation blends business, Mamma's Milkbar, thank you for changing women's breastfeeding lives for the better, Wendy Wei Xin Poon. To the talented Charlotte Clements, creative visionary behind Photography business Olive & Pop, thank you for your time and overall for bringing mothers' stories to life, for helping us to shine in our best light even when we feel we are experiencing dark days.

An extremely special thanks goes to my own mother, Cheryl Lewis, who showed me what it means to be a mother and shaped me into the person I am today. You taught me so much about motherhood by example. Your love, patience, and selflessness are qualities I aspire to every day, and I am blessed to have you as my role model. Also, thank you to my aunt, my other mother, Daryl Lewin-Burt, for your unwavering love and support throughout my life. I count myself exceptionally lucky to have the two of you in my life.

And to my mothers that have come into my life through other means, step-mother, mother-in-law, and 'surrogate' mother, thank you Charmaine, Jill and Georgie for shaping my life and mothering me as well.

I am also grateful to all my close friends who have provided their time, patience, and continual support of my dreams, and always encouraged me to pursue my goals. Thank you for cheering me along in my pursuit to spread the word of embracing the wildness of motherhood and a huge thanks to those of you who have offered your time regarding giving me feedback on my ventures related to this. You know who you are, thank you!

And most importantly, to my wonderful husband and rock, David Findlay, who stands by all my weird and wild creative ideas and endeavours, and supports our family like no other. To my sweet, sweet children, Harrison and Taylor, regardless of the challenges it takes to raise you, and the wild days we have together, the good will always outweigh these. You give me the ultimate reason for living and for striving to achieve, to show you that you can do ANYTHING you set your mind to. This is for you both. Thank you for being the light of my life and the inspiration behind this book. I love you more than words can say, and thank you for choosing me to be your wild mumma! **Here's to living all the wild beginnings with you both, always and forever.**

Pip Findlay **xox**

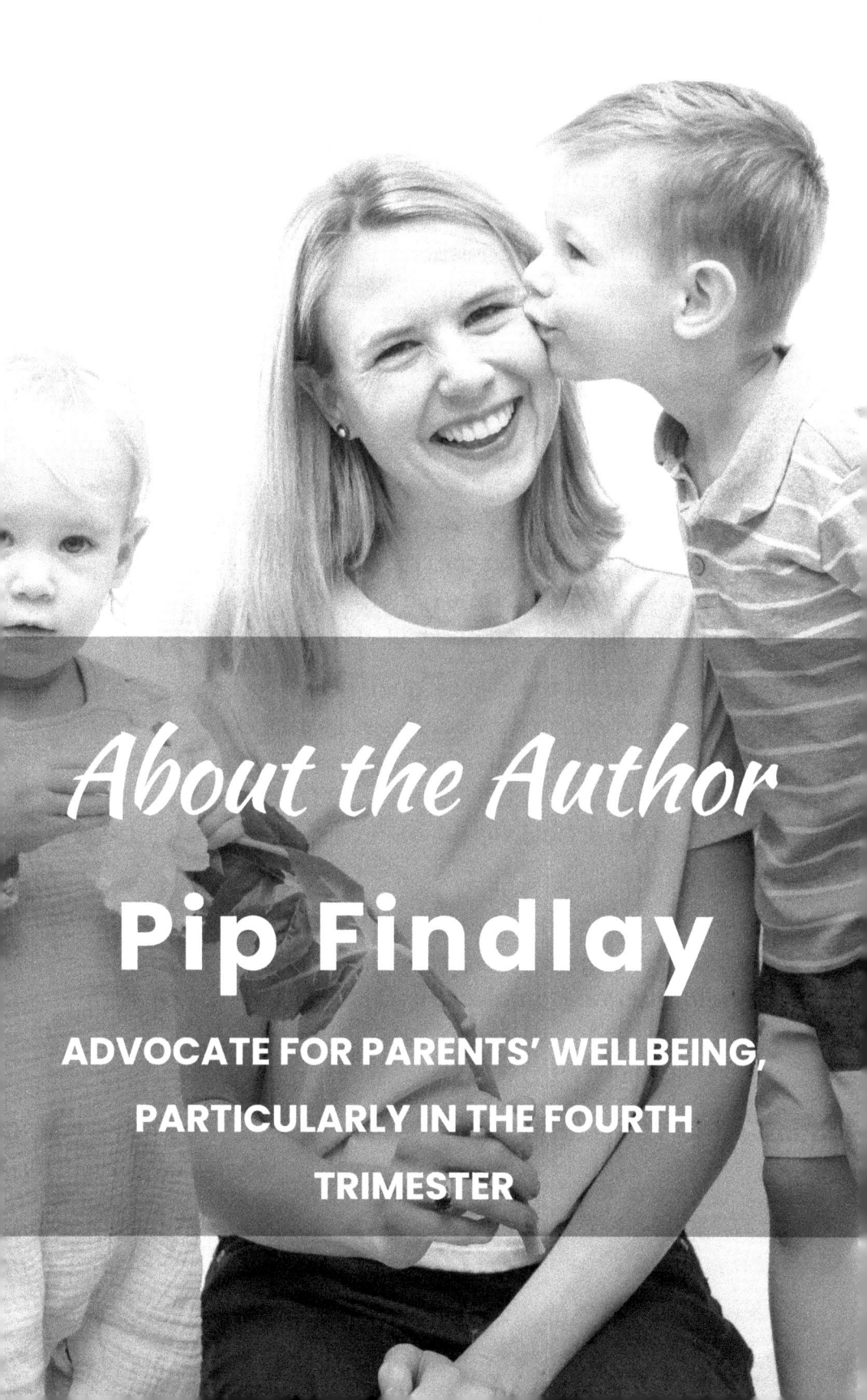

About the Author

Pip Findlay

ADVOCATE FOR PARENTS' WELLBEING, PARTICULARLY IN THE FOURTH TRIMESTER

As a former Parenting Educator and the Founder of Wild Beginnings, Pip has worked with New Zealand's largest Parenting Education organisation, Parents Centre Aotearoa, and she has educated hundreds of new parents to help them smoothly transition into parenthood.

To help her navigate this new wild world of parenting, Pip sought out trusted parenting experts in both New Zealand and abroad to support her role as the primary caregiver and to help her understand what was happening to her mind and body. Through this support network she was able to rebuild herself during the postpartum period and was far better prepared when she became a mother of two being able to thrive in her motherhood and feel truly empowered.

Pip has distilled all the advice, guidance and support she received into helping new parents start their own journeys through her 'Being a Parent' and 'All About You' workshops, online courses, and book, 'Into the Wilds of Parenthood: The Ultimate Survival Guide for New Mums Entering the Wild World of Parenthood.'

To learn more from Pip, follow her on Insta or Facebook **@wildbeginningsnz**, or drop her a message at **heywildmumma@gmail.com.**

What new parents say about Pip's classes and online courses

"We really enjoyed the class, Pip! Thanks for normalising some of the things that don't typically get talked about during this challenging time. It was great to hear a lot of relatable stories that made us feel a lot less guilty about some of the emotions we have experienced. Good to understand why we may have been feeling this way."

— Steven & MJ, Auckland, NZ.

"It was a really well-run session, thank you. I found it so valuable to share our experiences and learning about postpartum challenges and the science behind it."

— Annalise, Dunedin, NZ.

"I'm a new parent, my daughter Jasmine is 6 weeks old. I'm so pleased I found this course, as so much of what I've been looking at is all about the baby and what she should be doing at each stage. I definitely had the baby blues at the beginning and I'm keeping track of myself to make sure it doesn't go any further than that, but it's so nice to have something that's more focused on what this new journey is like for parents. I've shared the Being a Parent course with the rest of my antenatal class too!"

– Trina, Wellington, NZ.

"I'm going through the video modules casually and am really enjoying the topics covered and the realistic emotions to go with them. Thanks for putting together a really useful set of videos, giving new parents reassurance on their newborn path and not feeling alone along the way."

–Juliette, Tirau, NZ.

"Thanks so much for this very helpful workshop. Even though bubba has not been born yet, I feel much more confident for the first few weeks after talking/listening to you and the other fresh mums. This is great support! It was a very nice, safe environment for me, an easy-going atmosphere with motivation for me to be a part of the discussions. I gained some useful tips regarding the first days postpartum, coming home from the hospital and getting back into normal life at home with baby."

– Valeria, Waiheke Island, NZ.

"Pip has a warm approach and was able to establish rapport really quickly with the group, even though it was online. This made it a lot easier for women to share experiences with each other. This was a really helpful workshop to have at the beginning of being a mum and to know that everything I'm going through is normal and okay. Thank you!"

– Ally, Tauranga, NZ.

"Thank you for the wonderful presentation yesterday. It was very useful information and a great insight to motherhood and what it will be like."

— Elena, Wellington, NZ.

"I thought your session was great thanks & love the online course so I can go through things again when I need."

— Rachael, Auckland, NZ.

"Pip facilitated the zoom call well, it's not an easy thing to do! She encouraged discussion, while not putting people on the spot when they didn't want to talk. I found the discussion about what's 'normal' during the postpartum recovery period particularly helpful. Thank you very much for an enjoyable session."

— Sarah R., Auckland, NZ.

"I really enjoyed the class. It made me more aware of the tools and resources available to me and my baby. Pip was really nice and approachable."

— Sam, Auckland, NZ.

"Sharing what we were finding difficult as a group was great, it helped us see the challenges of motherhood and know that what we were all feeling is normal. Pip was really lovely and open."

— Michelle S., Auckland, NZ.

"The group discussion about what how we were finding the fourth trimester was so valuable, and the slides were great. Pip was fantastic, she made us all feel at ease so that we all felt comfortable to open up and as a result we got a lot more from the session. I appreciate her reaching out to me after the session to check I was OK too."

—Amy, Auckland, NZ.

"I enjoy that you share your own experiences and appreciated that you were comfortable enough to do this with my partner, Josh, present. I feel like a barrier to a lot of learning is that mums are apprehensive to share the good, the bad and the ugly and you shared it all. I really like hearing other people's stories."

— Abbie & Josh, Auckland, NZ.

"Pip is an absolute gem and the course so far has been extremely informative. I've learnt a lot of information that I wouldn't have known without her. Grateful for her knowledge, support and experience in this new journey of being a mum! Thank you Pip x."

— Krystle, Auckland, NZ.

"This workshop was the most valuable preparation for bubs impending arrival presented by one of the most amazing, selfless & inspirational mummas. It covers everything you 'don't know you need to know' about entering Motherhood; and discusses the not-so-rosy stuff about becoming a new mum that no one usually talks about. Learned about all sorts of topics from managing relationships in your new roles as parents, women's health physio and postnatal WOF, dealing with identity changes, mum guilt and so much more.

It armed me with new-found knowledge and awareness about what to expect, and methods to deal with that, so I was able to replace my apprehension with confidence and felt empowered to begin the journey of Motherhood."

— Michelle W., Auckland, NZ.

"I loved the class & the iceberg diagram was particularly helpful. It was great to get a focused overview of the postpartum period and the Fourth Trimester."

– Anonymous, NZ.

"I really enjoyed the discussion around 'Happy baby, happy parent' and the unrealistic expectations we can place upon ourselves, this was very helpful. It was also great to hear about what generally happens once baby will arrive and how things will likely affect me, before him arriving. I also liked knowing about safely getting back into exercise."

– Anonymous, NZ.

"I really liked Pip, she seemed super lovely, and I found her very relatable and knowledgeable. I liked the knowledge and preparation for the Fourth Trimester, something I find is only recently being explored and normalised."

– Anonymous, NZ.

"Thanks for doing a separate class for us! It was a great overview, and made us more confident in entering parenthood. I loved Pip's down-to-earth attitude."

- Anonymous, NZ.

"Pip has a warm and non-judgmental approach which is so welcoming at a time when lots of mums-to-be are feeling under pressure and overwhelmed by all the information and choices they need to make. Pip's passion for supporting mums to make the right choices for them really shines through. I particularly enjoyed the shared experiences of what other mums had found difficult, the tips re what to prepare for and after birth, and the postpartum plan."

– Sarah, Auckland, NZ.

"I love connecting with other moms and this platform allows this connection in a real and safe way."

– Sam, Auckland, NZ.

"This session was great because you need a support network to help you navigate motherhood. Google may appear to have all the answers, but connecting with fellow mums that have been through it makes all the difference; they are encouraging, reassuring and offer you love."

— Yael, South Africa.

"I liked the way Pip was an active listener and spoke to each individual like she understood where they were coming from. She did not judge anyone but encouraged them."

— Jasdeep, Auckland, NZ.

"It was really great to hear your personal experience, Pip. You were lovely, Pip."

— Rene, Auckland, NZ.

"Hey Pip! Thanks for the course yesterday it was great!"

— Ellen, NZ.

ADDITIONAL RESOURCES FROM PIP

If you liked the book, check out these online courses

① FREE Postpartum Plan

Prepare for entering parenthood with our FREE, downloadable postpartum plan! Crafted for meaningful discussions with your partner, this guide ensures alignment in the whirlwind of newborn care. While you can't effectively plan for your birth, you can for your postpartum!

Build your personalized postpartum plan, setting the stage for your smooth transition into this wild chapter of parenthood. Download it now and embark on this joint exploration to navigate the adventure together.

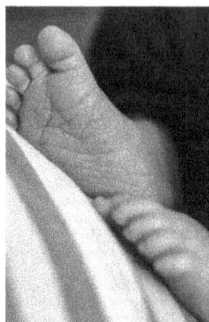

② Being a Parent Course

Introducing the "Being a Parent" course — an invaluable complement to the book that seamlessly enhances your learning and grants you access to Pip's expert guidance, directly from the experts themselves!

Parenthood is a remarkable journey filled with complexity and fulfillment. This course, designed to go hand in hand with the book, ensures a comprehensive understanding of your unique transition into motherhood. Pip personally guides you through this transformative experience, focusing on your well-being as a newborn parent. As you navigate new emotional, physical, and relationship changes, the course supports your healing and rebuilding, empowering you to confidently embrace motherhood. Accessible on the go, you can even listen with headphones during walks with your little one. Embrace the adventure of parenthood with the "Being a Parent" course and begin thriving in your early days as a newfound parent alongside your precious bundle of joy.

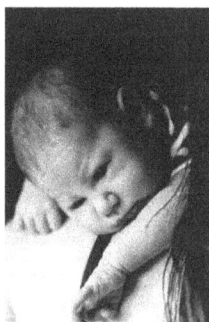

After more support? Grab the online courses at

wildbeginnings.thinkific.com

3 | The Fourth Trimester Survival Toolkit – straight from the Experts!

Crafted by the experts, this comprehensive course empowers rapid healing and transformation after childbirth.

Unlike the book, this immersive experience provides you with the actual resources directly supplied by the certified professionals themselves:

1. Navigate breastfeeding challenges under the guidance of an internationally certified lactation consultant and nurse, ensuring the best start to success with your feeding journey.
2. Nourish your body and your baby's development with simple, onehanded, lactation-friendly recipes provided by our nutritionist. Learn to make informed nutritional choices with her done-for-you shopping & nutritional literacy guides.
3. Rebuild and strengthen your body with safe-at-home exercises, courtesy of a senior pelvic floor therapist and postnatal certified personal trainer.
4. Cultivate thriving relationships with insights from a certified relationship and life coach. Learn to seek and accept help, navigate changing dynamics, and embrace personal growth so that you can reclaim your true identity.
5. Prioritize mental well-being and rest through guided meditations and self-care practices led by a somatic educator and instructor - actually sleep when the baby sleeps!
6. Understand your hormonal changes with specialized insights from a naturopathic doctor who specializes on women's hormones. Infographics and guidance help you comprehend these and communicate these changes to your partner so they can best support you.

Embrace the challenges and joys of postpartum. Embark on an empowered postpartum recovery today with "The Fourth Trimester Toolkit," and begin to thrive during this remarkable chapter of motherhood.

Your journey to well-being begins now.

After more support? Grab the online courses at
wildbeginnings.thinkific.com

Let's be friends

Learn more

**Website: Free postpartum Plan & Online courses
wildbeginnings.thinkific.com**

Facebook @wildbeginningsnz

Instagram @wildbeginningsnz

Email me at heywildmumma@gmail.com

THANK YOU

It's been my pleasure guiding you through your postpartum journey, and I wish you all the best in your postpartum recovery and your Fourth Trimester. Parenthood is wild, so get ready for the wildest, most beautiful, empowering journey of your life! I'm always here for you mumma, and I'd love to hear from you - be it via email, DMs, posts or more - keep me in the loop!

Lots of love

Pip xox